Gestapo Vo[lunteers]
The Upper Ca[rniola Home]
Defense Force
1943-1945

Axis Europa Books
53-20 207th Street,
Bayside, N.Y. 11364
USA

Gestapo Volunteers
The Upper Carnolia Home Defense Force
1943-1945

GESTAPO VOLUNTEERS:
The Upper Carnolia Home Defense Force
1943-1945

by Monika Kokalj Kocevar

Appendices & Editing: Antonio Munoz
English Translation:
Monika Kokalj Kocevar & Antonio J. Munoz

AXIS EUROPA BOOKS

UNIQUE BOOKS ON THE MILITARY HISTORY OF THE
AXIS FORCES, 1939-1945
53-20 207th Street, Bayside, NY 11364
fax orders: 1 (718) 229-1352
Phone Orders: (718) 423-9893
URL- http://www.axiseuropa.com

ISBN 1-891227-30-0

Book presentation & design: Antonio J. Munoz
Proof reading and Editing by Antonio Munoz,
Dust jacket design: Antonio Munoz
color plates: Darko Pavelic
b&w line drawings: Antonio Munoz

CONTENTS

GESTAPO VOLUNTEERS:
The Upper Carnolia Home Defense Force
1943-1945
Gorenjsko domobranstvo
(*Oberkrainer Selbstschutz*)

by Monika Kokalj Kocevar, MA

Introduction

The subject of the Slovene Home Guard and Home Defense force has almost been a taboo theme in Slovenia. For many years no research was allowed on this subject. The problem of Slovenian collaboration and the role of the Home Guard in actions alongside the German police and against the Slovenian [Communist] Partisans was always present. The *"Oberkrainer Selbstschutz"* (Upper Carnolia Home Defense Formation) was even less known than the history of the Slovene Home Guard. Many did not know that the Upper Carnolia Home Defense Force had its own formations and were completely independent of the regular Slovenian Home Guard. It was also thought that the whole formation numbered only a few hundred men.

After 1991, when Slovenia received its independence, attempts were made by many individuals to tell a different aspect of the Second World War in Slovenia. After 50 years people once again became interested in the war. They were no longer afraid to speak freely of the events which happened during World War II. With the aid of documents and written testimonies from numerous individuals, the researchers were able to make a survey of the situation as objectively as possible. In the post-Communist era not a lot of new archival material was found or new files opened to the public, but the access to different documents is less difficult, as one who wants to go through the documents does not need a special permission from the authorities. In addition, the archives of individuals, their stories and material were kept secret for 50+ years. The general government estimate as to the number of Slovenian victims lost in World War II during these past fifty years was about 50,000 – but current research has established that probably the number of actual losses was more like 70,000.

I began gathering information on the *Gorenjska* Home Defense Force back in 1990. All the data that I acquired was put into the computer program "Armida," which had been specially adapted for dealing with military formations. I was interested in the name and surname of each member of the Upper Carniola Home Defense *(Gorenjska samozaščita or Gorenjsko domobranstvo)*, date and place of birth, where the person lived during the war, his profession, which military formations the person joined (German army, Partisans, Home Defense) was he handed over to the Partisans in Carinthia in May 1945 and what was his ultimate fate.

I collected 3,792 names and surnames of men who were members of the *Gorenjska* Home Defense. Up until now it was estimated that the formation numbered about 2,500 men, but after going through all corresponding archival material and talking to many individuals I came up with a figure of 3,792. This is quite a large number in comparison with the Upper Carnolia Partisans who numbered 15,000 men and the majority of them were not in the units which operated in Upper Carnolia.

The work is based on this statistical data. The numbers are enlivened with many narratives. Very often I did not have any written records so I considered the recollections of those who survived the war and the tragic events after it. Although I agree with a British historian Max Beloff who quoted that *"an oral history is not a satisfactory substitute, since it relies on memory and no one's memory can be trusted"*[1]. Memory is sometimes very flexible but with a critical approach, the recollections can be very useful. In one of his books he presented a very true statement that *"the picture of events presented to the public is not and cannot be the whole truth; even if there is nothing particularly discreditable to hide, the characters in the story are rarely as single minded as they or their biographers would have us believe"*.

I must admit that the individual witnesses of the events whom I asked to tell their story, were not very talkative. The fear in them and distrust was still present. A part of the archival documents of the Upper Carnolia Home Defense which is at the disposal in the Institutes in Ljubljana was found in Kranj (Krainburg) just after the war. One of the men from Upper Carniola Home Defense told the Partisans where the Center Archives of the Upper Carnolia Home Defense was hidden. It was had been walled up in a house in Kranj. The Partisans took the documents but probably in the course of many years, the material was sent to different archives in Slovenia and probably also to other parts of Yugoslavia. The archive in Ljubljana presents only a small portion of the archive and the documents presented there are of a lesser importance. I learned from the conversation with those who were present in Carinthia that the whole

---

[1] Max Beloff, An Historian in the Twentieth Century, New Haven and London 1992, p. 24.

domobran archive was moved to Carinthia in May 1945 and was probably turned over to the Partisans. In the first transports sent back to Slovenia were also some carts containing archives and other documents.

I chose the title *Gorenjsko domobranstvo, Gorenjska* Home Guard, although the official name was *Oberkrainer Selbstschutz* in the German language or *Gorenjska samozaščita - Gorenjska* Home Defense. The organizers of the formation in Gorenjska wanted their formation to be named the *Gorenjsko domobranstvo* as the Home Guard in Ljubljana province had named their organization the *Slovensko domobranstvo* (Slovene Home Guard). Because, beginning with the title itself, it would be seen as a unit with more independence from the German occupier and more clearly understandable that they were not being used as an auxiliary police service which played the sub-servient role towards the Germans. Also they wanted to stress the formation's basic task- to defend homes.

The Home Defense wanted to collaborate with the Slovene Home Guard but the Germans did not allow this as they were afraid of a strongly united Slovenian military organization. The official forms and letters and even the seal of the unit from Upper Carniola, bore the name *"Gorenjsko domobranstvo"*, but was used only in correspondence between the Headquarters of the Home Defense and the various posts. The newspapers and magazines who wrote in favor of the new organization named the formation of *Gorenjska* Home Defense: *Samopomoč*-Selfdefense, *Brambovci*-militiamen, *Varnostna straža*-security guards. Partisans and their supporters used the expressions "White guard, the white, *Schwaba* guards, home burners".

The Situation in Slovenia and Upper Carnolia 1941 - 1943

On March 25th, 1941 the President of the Yugoslav government, Dragiša Cvetković and the Minister of Foreign affairs, Dr Aleksander Cincar-Marković signed in Vienna a treaty in which Yugoslavia joined the Tripartite Pact. Because of mass public disagreement to this pact, a group of officers whose commander was Dušan Simović forced the Cvetković government to resign and Simović was appointed Prime Minister. King Peter II was proclaimed to have come of age and was asked to take over the leadership of the state, but the new government did not retract the accession of the Tripactite Pact.

On April 6th, 1941 German units attacked Slovenia and the rest of Yugoslavia. The Italians in these first days only sent into Slovenia patrols and only later joined the German units in occupying the Slovene countryside. After the initial military operations the German

9

49th Mountain Corps took over the border passes into Austria - Jezerski vrh, Ljubelj and Korensko sedlo. Voluntary mobilization now began in the countryside. From Kranj, the center of Gorenjska, about 300 volunteers were sent to Novo mesto where they were joined by other 100 men from Jesenice, an industrial center in Gorenjska. Italian military activity was restricted only to the territory of the Julian Alps and the river Sava Dolinka. With the collaboration of a German Division, the Italian army took over Kranjska gora, Upper Carnolia, a well known vacation region visited by many Europeans even before World War II. Near Jesenice the Italians were stopped by a group of volunteers from that town, but this Slovenian group had to retreat because the regular army had already withdrawn. The units of the Yugoslav army demolished bridges over the river Sava near Radovljica and Kranj but nevertheless, on April 13th, 1941 the Italian army marched into Kranj and Škofja Loka. By April 14th, Slovenia was occupied.

Adolf Hitler divided Slovenia on April 12th, 1941 as per his instructions for the disintegration of Yugoslavia. The Slovene ban and the National council in Ljubljana tried to agree either with the Italians or Germans to form a new Slovenian state with a special status and within the framework of the axis forces, but were not successful. On April 17th a capitulation was signed and on April 20th the ban's domain and the National council ceased to exist as a political entity in the country.

Slovenia was dismembered among the Italian, German and Hungarian occupiers. Germany received the biggest part, getting the central and northern part of Slovenia (Upper Carnolia, Styria and a part of Slovenian Carinthia). The Italians got the southern part (with Lower Carnolia, Bela Krajina and Inner Carnolia) and the Hungarians received the small part in the extreme northeast which was incorporated into the Hungarian state on December 27th, 1941. The Italians formed from the occupied territory the Ljubljana Province, Provincia di Lubiana, and annexed it to the Italian state on May 3rd, 1941.

For Styria and Upper Carnolia, Hitler chose the same occupation system as for Alsatia, Luxembourg and Lorraine. Dr Siegfried Uberreither was made the provincial leader of the NSDAP in Styria and Franz Kutschera was appointed for Carinthia. They also led the civil administration and were directly subordinate to the Nazi Party leadership. Slovenian Styria was placed under the control of Uberreiter who assumed his responsibilities on April 14th, 1941 when he came to Maribor (Marburg). Franz Kutschera, responsable for Upper Carnolia, arrived in Bled sixteen days later, on April 30th when the Italian army withdrew to the right bank of the river Sava.

10

The Italian occupiers were not satisfied with the demarcation line but after the final agreements of the German-Italian boundary commission, whose final decision was reached on September 13th, 1941 the Italians had to submit to a decision that the western border would follow the line from Žiri, north from Polhov Gradec and south from Šentvid and Črnuče (in the suburb of Ljubljana). At the end of April 1941 Upper Carnolia was included into the 18th (Salzburg) Military Regional District "Alpenland". The head of the civil administration for Southern Carinthia appointed was Franz Kutschera. His headquarters was located at Bled (Veldes) until January 12th, 1942 and then was located in Klagenfurt, just across the border in Austria. NSDAP political commissars were appointed in all five Upper Carnolia districts and one commissar for Slovenian Carinthia and a part of Podravje. Nazi commissars were also organized in August of 1941 in Kranj, Radovljica and the Kamnik provincial districts. They were led by higher ranking NSDAP leaders who were renamed as state councilors on February 1st, 1942. The former district Ljutomer was on July 1st, 1941 annexed to the German Radgona district. From January 20th, 1942 the district Dravograd was divided between the provincial districts of Wolfsberg and Velikovec in Austrian Carinthia. This was one of the first goals the German occupier prepared for the Germanization of the Slovenes. Many libraries and archives were destroyed. Slovene books were sent to a special place in Kranj and then burnt. Printing of Slovene newspapers and magazines was prohibited. Personal names and surnames and names of villages were Germanized. The pre-war societies were dissolved. Slovene schools were closed down. German teachers came to Slovenia to organize German language courses at the end of August 1941. In December 1941 even the mountain peaks got German names. The [Catholic] Church property was confiscated and placed at the disposal to the state commissioner for reinforcing the Germanhood. Also confiscated was the property of the administration of former ban's domain. Germans prepared the plans to expel 80,000 to 100,000 people from their homes in Upper Carnolia. They also thought to expel the population from the 20km frontier border line with the Province of Ljubljana. The Commander of SD[2] and SIPO[3] was also the commander in charge of the expulsions. The German police came to Slovenenian Carinthia on April 15th, 1941 and to Upper Carinthia and Bled on April 20th. The commander of the SIPO and SD was SS-Obersturmbannfuehrer Fritz Volkenborn. His head-quarters remained at Bled until the spring of 1942. In the beginning of

---

[2] *Sicherheitsdienst*- German SS Security Service.- the Editor.
[3] *Sicherheitspolizei*- SS Security Police. - ibid.

11

June, 1942 Volkenborn was replaced by *SS-Sturmbannfuehrer* Dr Josef Vogt. In March, 1943 Vogt was in turn replaced by *SS-Obersturmbannfuehrer* Alois Persterer. In November, 1944 Persterer was replaced by *SS-Obersturmbannfuehrer* Karl Heinz Rux whose previous posting had been in Bromberg (Bydgoszcz) in Poland. Rux led the German police in Upper Carnolia until the end of war.[4]

Right after the occupation, the Germans put into prisons intellectuals, professors, government clerks and priests. Nearly all Upper Carnolian priests were expelled. Only the elderly were left in their priest's houses. Two camps for people who were about to be expelled were formed in Begunje and later in Šentvid (St. vid) near Ljubljana. From those camps railway transports sent the people to Croatia, Serbia or Germany. Three migration commissions had carried out racial and political searches of the population in Upper Carnolia from the beginning of April until the end of July, 1941. The majority got a very good racial mark and together with a political mark (estimation) they received the final marks which would decide their fate: "E" - to expel, "V"- to stay at home, or "A" – to move into the Reich proper[5].

The expulsions began on July 1st, 1941. At first the Germans expelled families from Radovljica. The first expellees were going on in Radovljica from July 1st-3rd 1941, then in Kamnik on the 5th, and on July 7th in Kranj. In the first transport, the German occupier expelled 522 people; from July 5th to 7th in five transports, more then 2,300 people were expelled to Serbia. Expulsions caused great alarm. Armed resistance and formation of the first Partisan groups now began which also helped to stop the expulsions, which were postponed until after the end of the war. Namely, the German police units had to operate against the Partisans and did not have time to completely expel the people at the same time.

A lot of people worked in the war industry and they were not expelled. Germans were surprised by what they considered a "good average racial mark" of people from Gorenjska. Those two facts were decisive, and in August 1941 the expulsions from this region were stopped. In the next years, the Germans expelled only the relatives of Partisans, in 31 transports of another 4,185 people who were sent to Germany. German violence intensified. On July 28th, 1941 a police curfew was introduced because of the activities of Partisan groups. A day after on July 29th, the head of the civil administration signed a decree forming a special court to deal with captured partisans. The head of the civil administration himself approved the death penalty.

---

[4] Tone Ferenc, Gestapo v Sloveniji, in Rupert Butler, Ilustrirana zgodovina gestapa, Murska Sobota 1998.
[5] Pre-war German and Austrian territory.- the Editor.

On July 22nd, 1941 a squad of Partisans from Rašica shot a former Yugoslav agent, the first mortal hit against the occupiers soldiers was recorded in the reports of the German propaganda office from Bled on July 16th, 1941. All *Gendarmerie* posts received the order for more severe security measures to be applied because of the sabotages and attempts on life of many individuals. Because of possession of guns was prohibited and sabotage activities took place, four hostages were shot on August 2nd, 1941. They were brought from Begunje prison, the largest prison institution in Gorenjska. On August 9th, ten hostages were shot because a member of the German SD was liquidated.

In 1941 133 hostages were shot. In 1942 the Germans shot in 48 groups a total of 612 hostages, and in 1943 in 19 groups 153 hostages. In 1944 in 28 groups, another 315 people were shot, and in 1945 in 10 groups 38 more hostages were killed. On September 20th, 1941 the Germans burnt down the village Rašica (10km north of Ljubljana) in return for an assault on a German car. In December, 1941 more houses were burnt in different villages of Upper Carnolia. On December 10th, 1941 the Partisan Cankar Battalion attacked the 2nd Platoon of the 181st German Reserve Police Battalion and killed 46 soldiers. In the first days of January 1942 more units of different German Police Battalions attacked the Cankar Batallion near the village Dražgoše. The Partisans withdrew from the village, in this struggle with the German police, nine Partisans were killed. The Police units burnt down the village, killed 41 locals, and expelled 81 people to the assembly camp in Šentvid near Ljubljana. Altogether 13 villages in Upper Carnolia were burnt down during the war.

The industry of Upper Carnolia worked for the German Army. The Germans intensively exploited the KIG (ironworks) at Jesenice, LGW - *Luftgewaerwerk* in Kranj which manufactured spare parts for airplanes, and produced magazine powder in Kamnik. 320 workers in a factory Titan Kamnik produced steel tablets for "Tiger" tanks and cartridges for mines. In the BPT factory in Tržič underwear, clothes, canvas and bandages for the soldiers was manufactured. In Lesce, a factory produced chains for armored tablets and caterpillars for tanks. The National Liberation Movement (OF- Osvobodilna fronta) tried to destroy these production facilities. Partisan units many times attacked those factories, and many employees went over to the Partisans and made lesser the efficiency of the plants by sabotaging them.

The head of the civil admistration, Franz Kutschera formed the *Kaertner Volksbund* on May 24th, 1941. In fear of any reppression, over 99% of the population enrolled into several Nazi organizations. Within this framework was also formed the *Wehrmannschaft* from

13

which it was planned to establish the units similar to the German SA[6]. Registering these units went very slowly, so by January, 1942 the total number of men in the *Wehrmannschaft* was about 17,000, and the final number would eventually reach 28,000 men. But they were not very efficient. Sometimes those units were only numbers on paper. In June, 1942 the *Wehrmannschaft* men had to return the uniforms to the German warehouses because quite a large number of them had gone over to the Partisan movement dressed in *Wehrmacht* uniforms. In October, 1942 the *Wehrmacht* units were officialy dismissed. From the Autumn of 1942 until April, 1943 the so-called *Selbstschutz* operated. They actually represented the reinforcements for the German *Gendarmerie* posts. Usually up to ten men from each village joined the *Gendarmerie* posts to do the patrolling together with the men from the post.

Friedrich Rainer was appointed in December 1941 as the new head of the civil administration. His first priority was to annex Gorenjska into the German Reich. The head of the civil administration in Styria, Uberreither, had the same orders. The annexation was postponed between October 1st to November 1st, 1941. Already the previous head of the civil administration, Kutschera could not carry out the given orders. The heads of civil administration in Bled and in Maribor (Styria was to be annexed into the German Reich at the same time as Upper Carnolia) wanted that the decree on the citizenship would be issued before the annexation of both provinces into the Reich would be performed.

In the new draft on annexation, which was prepared in the state offices in Berlin, the paragraphs on the citizenship and the way and time of introducing German law were left out. The annexation was then put off for January 1st, 1942 - probably to await for the new NSDAP gauleiter to arrive in Carinthia who would also be a German state deputy. Because of the Partisan attacks and concentration of Partisan units in Upper Carnolia, in addition to a lack of transports, the annexation was cancelled, then put off, so during the war it never came into reality. The province of Gorenjska and Štajerska were never a part of the Third Reich. In February, 1942 *Gauleiter* Rainer changed the name of Gorenjska from *Suedkaerten* to *Oberkrain*.

The German occupiers did not allow on their territory the formation of any Quisling formations. The Slovenes could collaborate with them as agents, trusted agents and reconnaissance men. In the summer 1942 the first *Gegenbands*[7] named *"Raztrganci"* began to operate. These

---

[6] *SA- Sturmabteilung.* The Nazi Party Storm Trooper battalions.- the Editor.

[7] *Gegenband-* Literaly means, "counter-gangs" or in this case, counter-insurgency bands.- the Editor

15

were Slovene men who helped German units to find the Partisan groups and destroy them. They were led and trained by the German *Gestapo.*[8] In the Kamnik district, the units were named **Martin**, while in the Kranj district, the unit was named **Ludwig**, and in Radovljica district, **Filip.** For special operations two other units, named **Štefan** and **Lux** were also available.

On September 27th, 1942 the majority of the people from Upper Carnolia who joined the *Kaertner Volksbund* received a special citizenship "a citizenship until recalled". The Germans had great plans in forming the NSDAP stormtrooper units which were mostly joined by Germans and ethnic-Germans. In 1944 the SA was incorporated into the German *Volkssturm*[9].

On July 7th, 1942 the Germans proclaimed mandatory work and military obligations. By 1944 more than 7,000 men from Upper Carnolia, who had been born between 1916 and 1926 were forcibly mobilized into the German army. From October 12th to 31st, 1942 men who were born in 1923 and 1924 were enlisted for work and military service. Men born from 1920 to 1925 were being enrolled from November 30th to December 19th, 1942. On July 1st, 1943 men born in 1926 were called up, and on December 1st, 1943 men born in 1927 were likewise summoned. Upper Carnolians fought for the Germans on the Eastern front and also in the west. A lot of them took part in the D-Day fighting, but on the German side. Many were caught and sent to England to the military camps where they formed a Partisan overseas unit and returned to their homeland. The men on the Eastern Front were less lucky. Many died in strong offensives, especially in the battle for the Crimea. Over 1,000 Upper Carnolia men were killed in action as German soldiers[10].

Desertions from the German army became numerous in the autumn of 1943, and in the spring of 1944 when men also began to join the Home Defense posts in Upper Carnolia. In April, 1941 there were only 140 communists in Upper Carnolia. After June 1st, 1941 the first military commitees were organized. They also prepared armed resistence. By the beginning of the resistance, 356 people came into the Partisan units there. The most organized was the uprising in the Kamnik area. In August, 1941 the "Storžič", "Cankar" and "Kamnik" Partisan Battalions were formed.

The Partisan leadership had called for an uprising in the winter of 1941-42, which was the most numerous in the Poljanska valley, north

---

[8] *Gestapo-* Short for *"Geheimstaatspolizei"* or State Secret Police.- ibid.

[9] *Volkssturm-* Peoples Army. The last levy of civilians into the Army.- ibid.

[10] Most likely under the German 336th Infantry Division / 49th Mountain Corps. – the Editor.

of Škofja Loka. At that time more squads and the "Prešern" Battalion were formed. In December, 1941 665 joined the Partisans in Upper Carnolia. The situation was very strained and the Germans formed "Police Operational Headquarters Southeast". Because of the German offensive in January, 1942 only 362 Partisans remained organized in these units. The rest went home or took shelter. The Partisan movement gathered new members in the Spring of 1942. The Slovene Partisan headquarters formed in April, 1942 the First Group of detachments, named "Gorenjski", "Kokrški" and "Koroški". The "Cankar" and "Poljane" Partisan Battalions were formed once again. The "Kamnik" and "Kokrški" Battalions were incorporated into the "Kokrški" Partisan Detachment. The units were decimated again in the German offensive "Enzian" which lasted from mid July to 27th September 1942[11]. On September 27th, Gauleiter Rainer proclaimed in Kranj (Krainburg) that Gorenjska was pacified (that meant that there were no bigger Partisan units in Gorenjska).

The western part of Upper Carnolia belonged to the Third Partisan operative zone, the eastern to the Fourth Partisan operative zone. On July 12th, 1943 the "Prešernova" Brigade was founded. It took part in destroying the village guard units at Turjak in Lower Carnolia. The Brigade was later incorporated into 31st Partisan Division. The "Gorenjski" Detachment was reformed in August, 1944 into the "Škofjeloški" Partisan Detachment and "Kokrški" Detachment and in the same month the "Jeseniško-bohinjski" Partisan Detachment was organized.

After the capitulation of Italy, the Germans sent additional units to the former Ljubljana province. On September 10th, 1943 the SS & Police Command founded two Operational Zones. Operationszone Adriatisches Kuestenland, and Operationszone Alpenvorland, and appointed provincial leaders of the NSDAP and state deputies Friedrich Rainer from Klagenfurt and Franz Hofer from Innsbruck. Adriatisches Kuestenland was composed of six provinces. The Ljubljana province was led by the President of the Provincial Administration, General Leon Rupnik. Rainer appointed also two Beraters (advisors), Erwin Roesener and Dr Herman Doujak. The German Police units in the province were answerable to the Hoeheren-SS und Polizeifuehrer (Higher-SS and Police Leader) in the 18th SS Military District under SS-Gruppenfuehrer Erwin Roesener and not to the Higher-SS and Police Leader – "Adriatic

---

[11] The newly formed Polizei-Gebirgsjager-Regiment 18 was the principal German unit used in this operation.- the Editor.

Coast" Region under Odilo Globocnik[12]. The Commander of the SIPO and SD from Upper Carnolia organized his branch office in Ljubljana.

For Upper Carnolia, by an order dated "September 30th, 1943" *Reichsfuehrer-SS* (National Leader of the SS and head of the German Police) Heinrich Himmler formed, in Ljubljana, an operational staff for destroying guerrilla bands, the *Fuehrungsstab fuer Bandenkaempfung*. It was led by Higher-SS and Police Leader Erwin Roesener, the head of the 18th SS Military District (Salzburg). The territories of Upper Carnolia and Lower Styria had been proclaimed *Bandenkampfgebiet*, ("Anti-Partisan Regions") on June 21st, 1943, and in December 1943 Himmler proclaimed the Adriatic Coast Region to be the territory of Partisan struggles as well.

The big German offensive *"Wolkenbruch"* ("Cloud Burst") began in November, 1943 in Upper Carnolia. Partisan units attacked the German posts. Only two companies of a German police regiment[13], the *1. Gendarmerie Bataillon (mot.)*, and *499. Reserve Grenadier Bataillon*[14] were in Škofja Loka, in the western half of Upper Carnolia. The Selška and Poljanska valley (north from Škofja Loka) were liberated in October, 1943. Also In October 1943 the valleys of Poljanska and Selška were liberated but in November the German offensive reoccupied these areas once again. On December 15th, 1943 the "Prešernova" Brigade suffered a great defeat in the Pokljuka Mountains. In the same mountains the 9th Partisan Corps was formed, which was raised to control the territory of Gorenjska and the Littoral.

In July 1942 the first meetings to organize village guards in Upper Carnolia took place. This meeting was held at Strmol Castle, 5 kilometers from Kranj[15]. Many notable civilian officials and wealthy landowners attended, as well as large businessmen, like the Lojze and Vitko Mejač brothers from Komenda, a lord of the manor from Rado Hribar and from Strmol and many others from Jesenice, Škofja Loka, Kranj and Kamnik, plus state councillor Janez Brodar from Predoslje also attented this meeting. The meeting was officiated by Dr Albin Šmajd, a lawyer from Radovljica and a state councillor.

The Partisan security and inteligence service (VOS) soon learned about this meeting and liquidated some of the attendees, most notably Mejač Brodar who was killed, while his brother Janez Brodar

---

[12] Odilo Globocnik's previous post in Lublin, Poland had been infamous. – the Editor.

[13] III.Bataillon/ SS-Polizeiregiment 24.- ibid.

[14] Stationed in Udine, in northeastern Italy – ibid.

[15] "Krainburg" in German.

fled to Austria. VOS began liquidations of influental business and civilian officials from Upper Carnolia for whom they thought they might have been the organizers of the White Guard, or later, the Home Guard, or if they were sure the locals would not want to cooperate with the Partisans. The "justifications"[16] reached their peak in 1943. Another shock to the Partisan movement were the activities of *SS-Hauptsturmfuehrer* Helmuth Rozumek. He came to Upper Carnolia as part of the SD and SIPO Command in Bled in April, 1942. He soon gained contacts with the local Partisan activist cell, pretending to be Anti-Nazi, and pro-Partisan orientated. He stated that he wanted to supply the Partisans and give them important information. The local Partisan command believed him until it was too late. Many men were arrested and killed because they were betrayed to the German police by Rozumek. He even had some connections and meetings with Partisan commanders of the 2nd Operational Zone in Upper Carnolia, and members of the Country Committee of the Communist Party of Slovenia. Some activists who associated with Rozumek were arrested and killed by the Gestapo when Rozumek did not need them any longer.

In mid-1943 a Chetnik committee for Upper Carnolia was organized. In the spring of 1943 an Upper Carnolian Chetnik detachment was founded in Polhograjski Dolomiti. The leader was Jože Hlebec. Among the Chetniks was also an army chaplain, France Malovrh who suggested that a group of men should go to Upper Carnolia, under Mežakla near Jesenice. The first group came to Žiri in June, 1943. They got in contact with a district secretary of the Liberation Front and stated that they wished to collaborate with the Partisans and move freely through the forests of the Poljanska Valley, but the negotiations never materialized. When Italy capitulated, the Upper Carnolian Chetnik detachment went to Vrhnika (about 30km south from Ljubljana) and joined the Slovene Home Guard post.

Already in November 1943 there were many preparations to organize a Home Defense post in Jesenice. At the end of 1943 the *Črna roka* (Black Hand), the illegal organization within the Home Guard, appeared. The Partisan Security Intelligence Service (VOS) liquidated almost all of the organizers. One of the leaders was Janko Soklič who ran away to Kranj. Nevertheless, the organisatfon of *Črna roka* began to operate in Jesenice. The first victims of the Black Hand were killled in December 1943. Seven Partisan activists were killed in Jesenice. In March 1944 the Black Hand killed six more people. Near the bodies were left lists with the emblem of the organization- a black hand. The civilian population was very disturbed by this, so in April

---

[16] i.e.- assasinations.

18

1944 the *Gestapo* prohibited the activities of the Black Hand, but in spite of this order, members continued with killings in all parts of Slovenia *until December 1944. Formation of the* Slovensko domobranstvo in Ljubljana province and the *Domobranstvo* in the Slovene Littoral.

After the capitulation of Italy, a Divisional General and later President of the Provincial Administration, Leon Rupnik, together with the Higher-SS and Police Leader of the 18th SS Military District, *SS-Gruppenfuehrer und Generalleutnant der Waffen-SS und der Polizei* Erwin Roesener, and Albin Šmajd, a lawyer from Gorenjska, decided to form a home guard to protect order and peace in Ljubljana province. The first battalion was formed from units of village guards and Chetniks from Zapotok. The Slovene newspapers published on September 24th, 1943 a proclamation that the Slovene Home Defense Legion had been formed.

They began to enlist new members on September 27th. Rupnik proclaimed himself the Commander of the Slovene Home Guard, while he appointed Colonel Anton Kokalj as "Inspector of the Home Guard". When Roesener returned to Ljubljana he did not confirm Rupnik to be the Commander. He even relieved him of duty. Rupnik was later appointed the "Inspector of the Slovene Home Guard," but all Home Guard units were in reality, answerable to Erwin Roesener. Later an initial batch of ten German officers and 20 N.C.O.'s arrived from Berlin who were to train the Home Guard. The officers were led by *Hauptmann der Schutzpolizei* (Captain of the Police) Erich Schumacher.

Although the *domobranci* wanted to fully mobilize into their own independent units, the German command insisted on volunteers. Roesener decided that the Slovene leadership was to be in charge of only organising activities, while the operational control of the Home Guard units were to be at the disposal of the German police unit commanders. In October 1943 an Organizational Staff was formed for the *Slovensko domobranstvo.* It was led by Franc Krener.The first posts of the Slovene *domobranstvo* were located from Postojna in the Slovene Littoral to Kostanjevica in Lower Carnolia. During the German offensive in the autumn of 1943, some Home Guard units participated.

In November 1943 the Partisans destroyed the home guard post in Grahovo. Since January 1st, 1944 the *Slovensko domobranstvo* was paid by the Higher Commissioner. Until the beginning of December of 1943 six (6) Home Guard battalions operated. Their duties were to protect villages and lines of communication. By the end of December, 1943 more combat units with headquarters in Ljubljana, Velike Lašče, Novo mesto and Polhograjski Dolomiti were formed. The Fifth

Combat Group[17] was to protect the railway between Ljubljana and Planina, while the Sixth Combat Group was in Kočevje, and the Seventh Combat Group in Grosuplje.

In February, 1944 a propaganda group of the Slovene Home Guard was sent to Upper Carnolia and the Littoral. On February 25th, the Organization Staff reorganized the Slovene combat groups into the following: (1) A School Group, (2) Combat Group for railway protection, and (3) a Combat Group for defending Novo mesto. In March, 1944 the First Assault Battalion was formed. In December, 1943 Rainer ordered that the police auxiliary units in the former Ljubljana Province (not in Gorenjska!) should take an oath. *Domobranci* swore twice, on 20th April 1944 and the others who enlisted to the *Slovensko domobranstvo* later, on January 30th, 1945. Both times the swearing in ceremony took place in Ljubljana and for other posts who were stationed outside Ljubljana, the oath-taking was also organized in Kočevje, Novo mesto and Velike Lašče.

In May, 1944 the Germans divided the whole territory of the former Ljubljana province into four defensive regions and in each was founded an Home Guard Assault Battalion. In the northern zone the battalion which was formed before, in Novo mesto, Battalion "O" operated. At Rakek W, Grosuplje M. Battalions assaulted the Partisan liberated territory.

Slovene home guard posts collaborated with the Upper Carnolia Home Defense units although the German occupier had actually forbidden this. Why? Probably because they were afraid that both organizations would become too strong. It is a fact that the Germans did not completely trust the Home Guard, and neither did the Home Guard completely trust the Germans. In November, 1943 the Slovene Home Guardsmen came all the way to Škofja Loka (about 25 km north from Ljubljana) and began to mobilize the men there. They could not pass the border of the former Ljubljana Province without having a special permission from their superiors (i.e.- the German command), although the Ljubljana Province did not exist formally the border crossing was still very strict. Even the Home Guard often could not get permision to visit their relatives in Gorenjska without German knowledge and approval.

The Slovenenian Home Guard quoted in their reports that the spring of 1944 was coming and that the Partisans would make mobilizations. They mentioned also the activities of the posts in Upper Carnolia where the Home Defense unit in Suhi Dol, Lučine, Gorenja vas and Črni Vrh were located. The 44th Company of the Slovene Home Guard patrolled also around the villages which territorialy belonged

---

[17] Also battalion in size.

to the Upper Carnolia Home Defence Force. Both, Slovene Home Guardsmen and men from the posts in Upper Carnolia even participated in actions together. In April, 1944 a group of *domobranci* from Rovte, together with *domobranci* from Suhi Dol and Lučine joined in with German units to attack the villages around Žiri, Gorenja vas and Št Jošt...one villager was quoted as saying: 'in Gorenja vas they were marching through the village singing dombran songs'.

The 43th Company from Horjul went to Kladje and Brebovnica and visited a post in Gorenja vas. With a decree from the Organization Staff, all the men in the Slovene Home Guard who were born or lived in Upper Carnolia were to be placed in a special register. Perhaps they were meant to be sent to the Upper Carnolia Home Defense posts. Leon Rupnik supported the Upper Carnolia Home Guard by sending cigarettes, books and propagandists, like his son Vuk Rupnik (who even brought machine guns) to these various posts. In October, 1944 Leon Rupnik continued to allow the support of domobran activities in Upper Carnolia, but only in the Spring of 1945 did General Roesener agree to send in some *domobranci* to organize the Home Defense in Upper Carnolia, and to release from prison the men who had organized the Home Defense in Gorenjska and were for those reasons sent to prison.

At a conference which took place at Bled from March 1st-3rd, 1945 General Rupnik expressed his desire to get permission to mobilize men into his units, but mobilization was allowed by Roesener only in the first days of May, 1945 when practically no men were left to be recruited[18]. But he issued a special order that the units from Upper Carnolia could be trained in Ljubljana. So only in the first days of May, 1945 was a united *domobranstvo* allowed to be formed.

The Slovene Home Guard and Slovene People's Party (SLS) also tried to organize the *domobranstvo* in the Littoral because the National Liberation Movement was very strong there. When Roesener cashiered Colonel Anton Kokalj, Kokalj went to Trieste and negotiated with the Higher-SS and Police Laeder for the Adriatic Coast, Odilo Globocnik and oferred to organize units there. At that time in the Littoral operated the *"Primorski"* Home Guard Detachment[19], which was sent there by Leon Rupnik. In December 1943 the detachment was subordinated to Anton Kokalj. On 26th November 1943 Globocnik founded the Slovene Littoral Home Guard, or SNVZ (The Slovene National Security Force), and appointed Kokalj as Inspector for Provincial Security in the Adriatic Littoral.

---

[18] The Partisans had seen to that by recruiting the men themselves!
[19] A battalion strengthed unit.

21

In October 1944 the formation was reorganized into the 1st Slovene Assault Regiment, with four battalions and supplementary support units. In the Vipava valley a Combat Group "Ajdovščina" was raised in March, 1945. The officers came from Ljubljana province. In Trieste a recruit school was located and in nearby Devin a school for officers and NCOs. The SNVZ numbered about 2,000 men. The Germans used the SNVZ units to patrol the territory. On September 1st, 1944 the units of the 9th Partisan Corps defeated the post at Črni vrh near Idrija. The Partisan victory met with a wide response. When the Slovene National Army was founded[20], Colonel Kokalj enlisted the NSVZ formation in it. That was very important because the domobranci counted on them when the allies would appear in the Slovene Littoral and the Littoral *domobranci* would make the first contacts with them. At the end of the war, Colonel Kokalj simply disappeared. Some SNVZ units withdrew to Friuli in Italy and saved thus saved themselves from Partisan retribution.

In the units of the Upper Carnolia Home Defense there were some men who were born in the Littoral but there is no proof that the formation of Littoral Home Guard and Upper Carnolia Home Defense ever collaborated jointly in any operations.

Establishment of the Posts in Upper Carnolia

The Upper Carnolian Home Defense collaborated with different organisations and individuals. As has already been stated, the organizers did not have much luck in organizing the Village Guard units in 1942 and 1943 in Gorenjska. Some people were killed by the Partisan Security and Intelligence Service, and Janez Brodar fled to Vienna, while Albin Šmajd ran away to Ljubljana. To find the roots of the initial organziation of the Gorenjsko domobranstvo it is necessary to go a few years back.

The SLS was organized on May 29th, 1941. It was a semi-military, illegal organization whose initials stood for Slovenska legija (Slovene League). After the Yugoslav collapse, this secret organization tried to attack the former members of the Association of Young Men Sections, or "Zavan fantovskih odsekov". The members of the Slovene League swore that they would work for liberty and the independence of Slovenia. The leaders of the Yugoslav National Party, were liberals and fought for the centralization of Yugoslavia, whereas SLS wanted more autonomy for Slovenia within Yugoslavia.

---

[20] This was a last-minute act of desperation, declared on May 4th, 1945 by the Slovene Nationalist who were hoping that the western Allies may aid them against the [Communist] Partsians.

Thus the SLS and the YNP were at odds with one another. The SLS organized the Sokolska legija (Falcon League), and the different groups, among them also Stara pravda organized the Narodno legijo (Natioanl League).

The SLS was organized on traditions of good relation with the Catholic Church, within the framework of religious, cultural, educational, and economic activities which would influence all spheres of man's life. Even before the start of the Second World War, political Catholicism had been formed. The leaders were aware of the need for reforms in the field of social welfare, and for keeping the Slovenenian workers within the Catholic community. They found the solution by collaborating with Catholic Action, the most active group within the Catholic movement for reorganization of the life of the Slovenian people based on Catholic principles.

There was even a young men section and young girls club within Catholic Action. They strived for Catholic principles in public life, the schools and the economy. Their ideal was to keep loyal to the Slovenian nation. SLS spoke in favour of nationality very tightly associated with Catholicism. In the Spring of 1942 the Slovene Alliance was founded. It was supposed to settle matters and relations between the Slovene League and semi-legal, political and semi-military movements. Following the instructions from London, the alliance had to acknowledge the Chetnik General Draže Mihailović. Slovene Major Karel Novak was Mihailović's reperesentative in Slovenia, and formed the initial Chetnik groups. The Slovene League later only formaly joined the Chetnik movement. Above all they supported their political ideals- a new state for Yugoslavia with the help of the western allies.

On September 22nd, 1943 the SLS founded in Ljubljana an Anti-Communist board. Its president was the leader of the Slovene League, Jože Sodja. The committee asked Leon Rupnik to establish the *Slovenska domobranska legija*, or Slovene Home Guard League. Each of the two leagues, the Slovene and Sokolska League, had their own Intelligence Service. General Rupnik merged the intelligence office with the Slovene league's counterpart into the Intelligence Office of Provincial Administration. This state intelligence service was very heterogenuous. One group did not want to be tied to any political party, spoke in favour of the Slovenenian nation, and was loyal to the Germans. It was led by Leon Rupnik, the other tied itself to the Chetnik movement and tried to be prepared for the moment when the "Slovene National Army" would join the western Allies.

All the members of the Slovene League swore they would act against the occupier. The State Intelligence Service was led by Vladimir Vauhnik. The *Slovenska legija* and *Sokolska legija* sent, in the

23

autumn of 1944, men to Uppper Carnolia to the Home Defense posts. Quite a number of them became the commanders of the posts. They were persuaded by Milko Pirih and Janez Grum to leave their post and go to Gorenjska. Milko Pirih was a commander of a Slovene Home Guard post in Dravlje, in the northern suburbs of Ljubljana. In one of his letters Milko Pirih wrote to Mirko Bitenc that the Chetnik movement led the Upper Carnolian Home Defense and stated that *"If Rupnik and his son want to succeed they would not be able to go past their organization in this moment to link up spitualy and military. A year of our work in Upper Carnolia cannot be surpassed by a few days' work, although done by Rupnik... Please try to explain to General Rupnik the situation in Upper Carnolia"[21]*. Mirko Bitenc was an officer in the Home Guard and one of the leaders of the Chetnik movement in Slovenia.

Because of their activities, especially in trying to establish contacts with the western Allies, some of these men were arrested in February, 1945 by the Gestapo, while some were also sent to Dachau concentration camp. As I've stated before, Leon Rupnik and Roesener discussed their fate. The *Slovenska legija and Sokolska legija* argued again when both of their members were to be incorporated into the "Slovene National Army". The Slovene league stated that they could not be compared with the job of individuals from their league who joined the posts in Upper Carnolia, and lived in danger with the work done by members of *Sokolska legija* who spent the war in as an illegal organization in Ljubljana. In spite of this, both organization's members were to be treated equally.

In the beginning of 1944 also the locals population from Upper Carnolia started to organize posts on their own. The situation was quite favorable. In Upper Carnolial the Partisan units were not as numerous, and former politicians were again very active - Janez Ovsenik from Predoslje, and the Dean in Kranj Matija Škerbec. Dr Albin Šmajd tried to persuade Janez Brodar to return to Slovenia. Brodar had been living in Vienna since 1942. He was born in 1885 and was politicaly active since the Great War. In the Kingdom of Yugoslavia he had been a deputy and a senator. He had three sons. Two of them were Home Guardsmen, one was also a commander of a Home Defense post in Gorenjska.

Members of the SLS from Ljubljana also took an interest in forming a Home Guard formation in Uppper Carnolia. On February 17th, 1944 a Provincial Committee for Gorenjska was founded in Ljubljana. Dr Albin Šmajd was the President, Dr. Jože Lavrič, a secretary of Rural chamber, was appointed its Secretary, Dr. Anton Megušar, a lawyer

---

[21] Vestnik, 1985/2, Buenos Aires 1985, p. 163.

from Kranj and Dr. Tine Debeljak, a writer and an editor of the cultural page of the SLS magazine, Slovenec were the members of the board.

At that time the Germans were prepared to allow units which would help in an auxiliary police fashion to maintain order and security and protect the war industry. More and more men came on furlough from the German army and had no intention of going back. The conditions to establish the Upper Carnolia Home Defense Force were given.

The German occupier had, besides the *Ordnungspolizei,* the regular (uniformed) Police and *Gendarmerie* (rural police) units, about 600 men from other units which came and left when necessary. In Kranj was the headquarters of the *28. SS u. Polizeiregiment "Todt",* which had arrived from Poland in February, 1944[22]. It numbered about 3,600 men. In July, 1944 the *"Alarm" Regiment* from the *Brandenburg Division* arrived, and established its headquarters in Bled, Veldes. There was also the *Landesschutzen-Regiments-Stab 184.* (Regional Defense Regimental Headquarters No.184[23]), which was part of *Division Nr. 438*[24]. Sixteen companies of the 184th Regiment numbered 2,600 men. Between June and September, 1944 a special SS hunter battalion arrived in Gorenjska[25]. Over 10,000 soldiers fought on the German side[26]. For a comparison, the Partisan units in Gorenjska only numbered about 700 men in the summer of 1944.

---

[22] At this time, the commander of this regiment was Oberstleutnant der Schutzpolizei Koesterbeck.- "The German Police" Axis Europa Books: Bayside, NY, 1996. Section "M", page19.

[23] Which contained the 517th, 927th, & 928th Regional Defense Battalions.

[24] This division was established in Klagenfurt on November 1st, 1943 and was subordinate to the 18th German Military District. In December, 1943 this division had the following units: Landeschutzen-Regiment 184 [Krainburg]; Landeschutzen-Regiment 18 [Cilli]; Grenz-Wach-Abschnitt XVIII [Villach] (Frontier Post Commands XVIII-C, XVIII-D and Regional Defense Battalion 721); and Grenz-Wach-und-Abschnitt XVIII-E [Pettau].

[25] The author could here be referring to one of two SS Jagdkommandos which operated under the heading of the 24th SS Karstjager Division (later downgraded to brigade level). This formation never achieved divisional strength and when it fought in the field it was basically in two "hunter" groups. Since the unit operated along the Italo-Slovene frontier, the author could be referring to one of these groups. – the Editor.

[26] The "Alarm Regiment Brandenburg" was in reality the Brandenburg Training Regiment which had been shifted by the Wehrmacht Operations Staff on June 9th, 1944 to the area under the control of the 18th SS Military District. The regimental units were deployed as follows: Alarm Regiment Headquarters was at Bled (Veldes). The commanding officer of the Regiment was Oberstleutnant

Among the local founders of the Home Defense in Kranj were Franc Erpič, Milan Amon and Franc Šenk. They received permission from the SD and SIPO Command in Bled (Veldes) that they were allowed to organize a unit of the Upper Carnolia Home Defense force. The *Gestapo* warned them that they were not supposed to have any contacts with the Slovenian *domobranci* in Ljubljana. The group was given four barracks behind the Ika Factory and in front of the Kranj Sports Grounds. Every evening some *Gestapo* men came to guard these newly established installations. The organizers established the conditions under which they were prepared to operate. They were to command the units in the Slovene language, all Slovenians in the German army were to be discharged and sent to the *Gorenjsko domobranstvo*, and forthwith hostages would no longer be shot.

Apparently, during the period from August 1942 to February 1943 the Germans didn't shoot any hostages in Upper Carnolia, and from the concentration camps, men who wanted to join the *domobranstvo* were released, but the desires of the Slovenian organizers mostly remained mere wishes.

German authorities did not allow Slovenian deserters from the German army to join the domobranci but the head of the *Gorenjsko domobranstvo, SS-Oberscharfuehrer* Erich Dichtl suggested they should be registered under fictitious names. The posts carried out different ways to register the volunteers. Many different notices were sent to the post reporting where certain people were hiding. The domobranci came and took the men with them, so everything looked as if the men were forcibly mobilized into the domobranstvo. The Germans did not trust the *domobranci* and neither did the domobranci trust the Germans. Dichtl, who was Austrian by birth, was the exception to this rule because he had learned the Slovene language and had helped the domobranci on several occasions.

Germans never officially allowed former Slovenes serving as German soldiers from Gorenjska to join the *domobranci*. The Home Guard Post in Kranj even as late as in March, 1945 had problems with the *Gestapo* units from Kranj who would come to the post to try and arrest any Slovene deserters from the German army. The men from the post were prepared to shoot at the Gestapo. By the order of the

---

Martin. The 18th Heavy Weapons Training Company was stationed at Bled; The Ist Battalion was also at Bled & Freiburg; while the IInd Battalion was sent to St. Veit (on the Sava River). The IIIrd Battalion was sent to Stein, while the IVth Battalion under Oberleutnant Bostrick was quartered at Domzale-Hannsburg (NW of Ljubljana). The Regiment remained in this region until April 20th, 1944 when it was pulled out and transferred to Stockerau. – ibid.

local Home Guard Commander, they were directed to aim their guns at the two *Gestapo* cars which had arrived at their Home Guard headquarters in late March. There were some very tense and trying minutes, but the *Gestapo* men, upon seeing that they were going to be challenged, eventually returned to their cars and withdrew to their headquarters, never to return to the *domobranci* headquarters again. It is interesting that the Germans never pursued former Partisans who were known to be at the *domobranci* posts (and the lists of members contained also the data, the details of register of the German army and the Partisan movement!).

In May 1944 the SLS sent Slavko Krek, a nephew of former minister Miha Krek, to collect information on the conditions in Upper Carnolia, to reorganize the domobranstvo according to the instructions from SLS, and to help form and unite all Slovene military leadership. Above all, he was charged with helping to protect the domobran posts from more German influence. He received confidential intelligence data from Jože Sodja. Krek introduced himself as a General Rupnik's secretary and got in touch with Janez Brodar (at that time still in Austria) and Janez Ovsenik. Krek organized an intelligence service network which was especially well spread in the Kranj and Kamnik district.

Krek went also to Rudolf Humer in Škofja Loka who was appointed as liaison officer among the posts and was a fanatical Nazi adherent. He introduced Krek to Walter Hochsteiner, leader of the NSDAP in the Kranj district. In the spring of 1944, the *Gestapo* arrested Dr Albin Šmajd and confined him to Salzburg, Austria. Some other organizers were also arrested because they wanted to collaborate with the western Allies and their actions had been exposed by the Gestapo. It was thus important that Janez Brodar should return home. An agent of the Chetnik movement had approached him with a letter written by the SLS leaders in which they asked him to return to Slovenia.

In the summer of 1944, Slavko Krek went to Vienna, visited Brodar and tried to persuade him to take over the political leadership of the Upper Carnoliaa Home Defense Force because no headquarters for the formation had been formed. Krek also met Šmajd who gave him a task to organize an illegal organization. Šmajd then returned to Kranj and then to Ljubljana using Upper Carnolia Home Defense documents and under a fictitious name. In September, 1944 Dr Friedrich Rainer and Janez Brodar met in Carinthia near Woerther See in Austria. Soon after, Brodar came to Kranj and on September 17th, 1944 he made a speech in Trstenik, about 30 kilometers from Kranj. He spoke of the Home Guards and the (atheistic) communists. Brodar stayed with the *domobranci* at the Kranj post because it was safer for him. He also had an office there as well as one in Klagenfurt,

27

which was used for Upper Carnolians who returned from the German army. In mid-1944 the registration for conscription of men from Upper Carnolia into the German Army ceased.

Other organizers often made propaganda speeches in public, especially Rudolf Humer, Janez Ovsenik, Franc Erpič and Franc Šenk. In October, 1944 the organizers from Upper Carnolia- Janez Brodar, Janez Ovsenik, Slavko Krek and seven other members of the SLS met in a villa in Savnik by Kranj and discussed the details of organizing the illegal groups within Home Defense. They stressed the conspiracy towards the Gestapo and decided to organize groups of three men who would collect information for the Intelligence Service. Especially active was Janez Ovsenik. They divided Upper Carnolia into five districts and prepared groups who would act illegally.

That had already been the system of operational groups in the Slovene League in 1942. The provincial committee consisted of the president, Janez Brodar, Janez Ovsenik who was in charge of the Intelligence Service, and Alojz Perne who led Propaganda Department. Together, these men represented the political head-quarters of the Upper Carnolian Home Defense Force. Perne's brother was an organizer of the Village Guards in Lower Carnolia, and was in September 1943, killed as an officer in Turjak, a castle where the Village Guard had withdrawn to and were defeated by the Partisans. Alojz Perne was a Partisan deserter.

At the same meeting they also talked about the Slovene deserters from the German army. The group needed only a photo and personal data of an individual and were able to prepare documents for him[27]. In October and November of 1944 the activity of the Home Defense posts increased. The Commander of the SD and SIPO from Veldes, Alois Poersterer ordered Krek that the *domobranci* should stress anti-Partisan activity and the struggle against the western allies. In October, 1944 Krek met Mirko Bitenc. Major Bitenc was the commander of Chetnik units. They called themselves the Yugoslav Army and illegaly prepared for the expected arrival of the Anglo – Americans[28]. Their plan was to introduce themselves as soldiers for freedom who were waiting to take over the leadership of the Slovenian Home Guard units. At this time, the Slovene League now also formally joined the Chetnik movement. Persterer many times said that for tactical reasons, he still supported the Home Defense but

---

[27] Archive of Republic Slovenia, Office III, former Historic archive of Ministry of Interior Affairs, Šmajd's archive.

[28] This "arrival," never materialized. But even if it had, it is extremely doubtful that the western Allies would have lent their support to the Chetniks who were, by October, 1944 – regarded (rightly or not) as Axis supporters.- the Editor.

in an opportune time, he would send them all to the front because he wanted soldiers and not some "clerical political army". Rudolf Messner, the commander of the *Gestapo Aussenstelle* (State Secret Police Branch) in Kranj sarcastically called them *"Kristus Kaempfer"* (*"fighters for Christ"*), because the Home Defense units were very much under the influence of the Catholic Church. The posts were also accessible to Gestapo agents who wanted closer ties between the *domobranstvo* and the Germans.

The Upper Carnolian Home Defense posts

From the end of 1943 to the first days of April, 1945 nearly 50 Posts were established for the Upper Carnolia Home Defense Force. The exact number of them cannot be specified, because in some posts the *domobranci* stayed for only a few days and for some posts we do not have enough data to state that they really existed. Sometimes a few *domobranci* were sent to German posts but the garrison was still the German post and not answerable to the *Gorenjsko domo-branstvo*. Bigger posts exercised control over smaller posts and represented the main posts. All main posts were subordinated to the *Gestapo Aussenstelle*. The SD and SIPO from Bled had a branch office in Radovljica (the commanders were Ludwig Vonderten, Hans Kirchbaumer, Friedrich Zimmer, Johann Bachinger and Alfred Schroeder).
In Kranj, the commanders of the SD & SIPO were Karel Bayreuther, Heinz Althaus, Josef Platzl and then Rudolf Messner who came from Styria. In Škofja Loka, the commanders were Eugen Hitzler, Josef Schindler, Karel Luther and Hans Friedt; While in Kamnik the commanders were Friedrich Zimmer, and Alfred John. In Jesenice it was *SD-Untersturmfuehrer* Clement Druschke and at Litija it was Reinhold Gerlach, Ernst Schmidt, Josef Maureder, Josef Kinkelin, and Georg Walcher[29]. A post in Litija was subordinated to the *Gestapo* post in Litija and was a main post to Kresnice and Vače. The *Gestapo* Aussenstelle (Branch) in Kamnik controlled Lahoviče, Mengeš Vodice, Moravče, Stahovica, Stranje and the Domžale post. Domžale was a main post to Dolsko and Šentvid pri Lukovici. The posts in Kranj, Bobovek, Brdo, Predoslje, Voklo, Cerklje, Smlednik, Kovor, Jezersko, Goriče, Tržič, Mavčiče and Tupalice belonged to the SIPO Branch Office in Kranj. The SIPO in Škofja Loka controlled Žabnica, Bitnje and Škofja Loka. The posts in Sopotnica and Sveti Križ were subordinated to the Škofja Loka post. A post from Brezje was a main

---

[29] Tone Ferenc, Gestapo v Sloveniji, in Robert Butler, Ilustrirana zgodovina gestapa, , Murska Sobota 1998, p. 224.

post to Ribno and Kamna Gorica and belonged under the control of the SIPO at Radovljica.

In December 1943 and January 1944 the first posts of the Upper Carnolian Home Defense were founded in Suhi Dol, Lučine, Gorenja vas and Črni Vrh. They were aided by the posts of the Slovensko domobranstvo from Šentjošt, Horjul, Polhov Gradec and Rovte, which were situated near the border between Gorenjska and the former Ljubljana province. To organize a posts on the other side of the border was probably the main interest of the locals and the Slovene Home Guard leadership. Those posts were under the control of *Grenzpolizei* (border customs guards) which were subordinated to the Ministry of Finance in Berlin, and also the four posts which were founded first were financially supported by the ministry and not by the Police as the other posts were in Gorenjska.

Until the end of the war the problem of financing those four posts was never settled. Mainly local men were organized on those posts. Quite a number of them were already registred at the Slovene Home Guard posts in the vicinity which were already in existence in the Autumn of 1943. After the local posts in Suhi Dol, Črni Vrh, Lučine and Gorenja vas had been organized, the men went back to their local posts. Even individuals from other parts of Gorenjska, mostly from the area around Kranj, came to those first posts.

Early in the Spring of 1944 the posts in Škofja Loka (March 15th) and Kranj (April 12th) were established. In the first days of February, 1944 a group from the Partisan Security and Inteligence Service (VOS) killed an SS man in Škofja Loka. In revenge, German soldiers shot 50 hostages from the nearby villages. On March 10th, 1944 organizers of the Home Defense met in Škofja Loka. Another meeting was held on March 15th. The Partisans learned about the meeting and came into the house, right in the midst of the organizers and their discussion. Within seconds, the Partisans killed 9 people, among them was a woman and a small child.

Just a few days later the other organizers asked the *Gestapo Aussenstelle* (Branch office of the Gestapo) to give them weapons to defend themselves against the Partisans, and a group of the Home Defense led by Rudolf Humer mobilised men in Škofja Loka. On the following day, Home Defense men from Črni Vrh and Šentvid near Ljubljana came to support them. From Škofja Loka some men went to nearby Žabnica to organize a new post. In February, 1945 they raised a post at Sveti Križ near Selce. Until the establishment of the Center of Home Defense, the post in Kranj was very much under the influence of the *Gestapo* from Kranj. The Commander of the *Gestapo Aussenstelle* there was *SS-Obersturmfuehrer* Rudolf Messner and *SS-Oberscharfuehrer* Erich Dichtl who visited the post nearly every day. The post was a sort of a training unit for the newcomers. Their members were sent to posts in Cerklje, Predoslje, Lahoviče, Voklo, Smlednik, Vodice, Lesce and Domžale.

Since November, 1944 they had accepted newcomers from other posts who did not have uniforms or possess weapons. They would train them and then send them off to different posts. The headquarters of the Home Guard in Kranj also later included the Headquarters Center of the *Gorenjsko domobranstvo*. In July, 1944 an article appeared in the newspaper Karawanken Bote which, among other things, said: *"As you know, there is a very strong post in Kranj. The members, all volunteers, do their job and happily march through the town. We must greet the fact that so many people of Kranj joined the Home defence."* This post was moved in February 1945 to Stražišče. The post in Cerklje was founded on May 17th, 1944 and the members reported: *"Since the post has been established our boys- all brave men, have been chasing communists."*

In June, 1944 a group of *domobranci* came from Gorenja vas to Hotavlje and set up a post. After a month Partisans attacked the post and destroyed it. In July, 1944 the posts in Voklo and Lesce were founded. But they were later moved to Brezje in October of the same year. The post in Šentvid near Ljubljana existed earlier, but written documents date the post from "September 1944". In July the leader of a post from Škofja Loka, Rudolf Humer was in a public rally in Šentvid and addressed the men inducing them to enroll in the Home Defense. One of the most active posts and as well one of the strongest, was the Domžale Home Defense Post, which was formed on August, 8th 1944.

The men from this post later helped to form the posts in Šentvid near Lukovica because the groups from the Domžale post could not patrol the Moravče Valley as it was too far away. One of the organizers was Anton Šimenc who with the help of the Home Defense from Kranj, established a post in Domžale which was a center for the Kamnik District. In August was a post was established in Smlednik and in January, 1945 Fifteen men went to the post at Preska. The Home Defense unit in Tržič left the town in the summer of 1944, and the men were sent to other posts, but half a year later a group of men from the Officer's Course from Brdo near Kranj returned to Tržič and set up a new post in February, 1945.

In October, 1944 a post in Bobovek was founded. Thirty men protected the successful tile factory located there. In the same month a post was established in Kovor near Tržič and a month later, in November 1944, the posts in Sopotnica nad Mavčiče were also formed. At the same time an Assault Company was established at the post in Kranj. The Assault Company was a mobile unit and it was attached to the German Police in Styria to fight in a German offensive against the liberated Partisan territory in Gornji Grad in January, 1945. They established four posts; in Stahovica, Ljubno, Luče and Županje njive. In their reports they stated that the local people were very much afraid of them, specially because the German Police was with them.

The Litija post was raised in January, 1945. Its major task and the task of the posts at Kresnice and Vače, was to chase the Partisan messengers who crossed the river Sava on their way to Lower Carnolia.

A post from Tupaliče from time to time left some men to the post in Stranje which moved to Mekinje in March, 1945. In March, 1945 the *domobranci* from Brdo moved to Stražišče because the members of *Volkssturm* came to that former castle of Prince Paul Karadjordjević and occupied it. In late April, 1945 as the war was winding down, the last Upper Carnolia Home Defense posts were being established. In Kokra some 30 men were organized and seemed eager to fight against the Partisans. The main plan of the Home Defense in the last days of April, 1945 was to organize posts as near to the Austrian border as possible.

In the district of Jesenice there were no Home Defense posts. The organizers there had all been killed in December, 1943 and the commander of *Gestapo Ausenstelle, SD-Untersturmfuehrer* Clement Druske did not want to allow the posts to be organized. But nevertheless, there were about 200 active Home Guards in civil defense, mostly refugees from Lower Carnolia who carried out Home Guard propaganda. At their meetings came also a propaganda officer from the nearby home defence post in Lesce. In Kamnik there was also no domobran post, although the were seven Home Defense men in a house in the center of Kamnik.

Location of the Gorenjsko Domobranstvo Posts

Sometimes it was quite difficult to set up a post. The only empty houses were priest's houses and public homes, and even if the people were prepared to accept the Home Defense men it was usually not a large enough place at one farm, so the men were housed in three or four houses, depending on the number of Home Defense per post. That was the situation in Gorenja vas and Suhi Dol. The posts were mostly located on the farms of Home Defense adherents (Bitnje, Hotavlje, Tupaliče, Goriče, Sopotnica, Vače), in schools (Dolsko, Voklo), Public homes (Cerklje, Škofja Loka), priest's houses (Lahovče, Kovor, Kresnice) or public houses (Domžale,

Stranje). In Tržic a place for the domobranci was prepared in the factory at Peko, which manufactured shoes; But then the mayor insisted that they had to leave the village. In Mekinje the domobranci were located in a nunnary and in Smlednik, in the castle. In Jarše the post was located in a hospital. In Vodice the men were in civil parish house.

The Kranj post which was very strongly armed was first housed in four barracks near the sport stadium and then in February, 1945 the men were moved to a public house and a priest's house in Stražišče. Posts were also situated in former German posts. When the Germans left the post, the Home Defense came and took over the dwellings. That was the situation at Jezersko, Preska and Kokra. Very often as soon as the Partisans got the notice that the domobranci would want to found a post in a certain village, they came and burnt or demolished the buildings in which the domobranci might have had their post. In this way a lot of churches and priest's houses were demolished.

Arming and Protecting the Posts

Home Defense posts received weapons from the Germans and some arms they seized from the Partisans. Erich Dichtl ordered the Home Defense commanders that they had to send each week with the weekly report also a list of all weapons with the calibre of each weapon listed. The data acquired that describes how the *Gorenjsko domobranstvo* were armed are mainly Partisan reports which very often exaggerated the numbers. Sometimes the domobranci from the Kranj post when they would organize a parade for propaganda reasons, would borrow arms from the local German post (so that everyone would see how well they were armed and with what type of gun). Afterwards they would return the weapons to the Germans.

The posts were often surrounded by a wire fence and bunkers. In Predoslje the *domobranci* practiced firing their weapons with Russian machine guns and in Tupaliče with English machine guns. Around the post in Predoslje were more bunkers made of soil, 35 *domobranci* had, besides their guns, one heavy and one light machine gun. In Predoslje they had one heavy and one light mortar, one heavy and eight light submachine guns, the other *domobranci* had Italian or French guns. In Škofja Loka they had one light mortar, eight machine guns, five light Bredas, and three Zbrojevke. Around the post were five wooden bunkers which were connected by trenches. In Kovor two bunkers protected the post. They also had a watch tower. Around the post was a five meter high wire fence and trenches. The windows in the building were wainscouted by sand. They had one light mortar, four machine guns, two Zbrojevka, one Breda, five sub machine guns and 50 German, Italian and Yugoslav grenades. In front of the Vodice post the *domobranci* put a machine gun from an American plane which had been shot down in the vicinity. In the first weeks just after they brought the machine gun an accident occurred. The men wanted to examine the gun and tried to shoot with it. At that moment the whole machine gun exploded but no one was killed.

At the Kranj post the domobranci had 4 machine guns, many submachine guns and carabines. The light weapons had 8mm ammunition. The post was protected by a bunker which was linked with a post. The *Domobranci* stated in a report from 18th to 22nd January, 1945 that they captured 4 machine guns, 1 submachine gun, 19 guns, 9 grenades and 10,000 cartridges of rifle ammunition.

In a statistic surwey for 25th November to 10th January 1945 they reported that they seized one 75mm howitzer, 112 guns, 36 sub machine guns, 53 hand grenades, 5 machine guns, 1 anti-tank gun, 2 light and 1 heavy mortar, 20 kg of English explosives, 19 pistols, 31 rucksacks, 13 heavymines, 550 cartridges for the gun and 520 pieces of cartridges for sub machine gun.

The Home Defense posts covered with their activities the lower part of Upper Carniola. The posts were territorially limited and operated only within their *Gestapo* strongholds *(Aussendienststelle)* and the Post territory. If they went to the territories outside their control they first informed the commander of the Home Defense post to which territory they were going. Each day the password was changed. It was in the German language and it was the same also for the German police. It happened that two Home Defense patrols met and they began shooting at each other and just then they indentified themselves with a password.

At least five men together went to patrol once or twice a day. Very often there were more night patrols than day patrols. The Partisans were very well informed of all Home Defense movements and the patrol many times had to change the direction. The posts also had to have strong protection. At the Kranj post, 12 guards always protected the post and the Center.

Some operations to some distant sites were led by the *Gestapo*. Usually there were about 40 to 60 men staying at the individual post. Bigger posts had more then 100 men. Those were posts in Domžale, Črni Vrh, Suhi Dol and Voklo. In Škofja Loka were more than 150 men. The Assault Company had 100 men and were posted at Brdo near Kranj when they were not in action. In January, 1945 at the Kranj post were 160 Home Defense men, while at Brdo there were 400, and at Žabnica there were 60 men. At Stražišče there was a company of 120 men, at Škofja Loka there were 100, while at

Gorenja vas the command had a strong company of 140 men. At Sopotnica 70 men were posted, at Smlednik, 40; And in April of 1945 at Brdo there were 124 men, and at Cerklje there were 123 men, while at Smlednik 60 men were posted. Also in April, 1945 the post at Tupaliče had 75 soldiers, the one in Kranj had 69, while the post at Domžale had a "respectable" 100 men, and at Vodice 55 men were posted. At the post in Tupaliče were registered at a certain time about 80 men, but the total number of men who served in this post from one time or another was 180. Apparently, after the men had been registered they were sent to other posts.

In March 1945 there were 85 men at the post in Smlednik, but the total number of men who ever enrolled at that post was 141. When a new post was raised the newly mobilized or volunteer Home Defense men were sent there and also skilled Home Defense men from other posts were sent to join them. The home guards at the post in Smlednik complained that they were not able to go into any action because the total number of members that the post had, was only 34 men. The report from the post Cerklje also quoted that the men who were to go to the new post in Jezersko were *"undisciplined and low-spirited"*[30].

Only eight days after the post in Litija was raised it already numbered 82 men. Smaller posts such as at Dolsko and Stahovica only had 30 members. The above numbers show that the German occupier did not want strong Home Defense posts and when the number of the men at the post came over 100 they transferred groups of ten men to other posts or they founded new ones. Especially when the end of war was approaching, the new posts did not have more than 30 men. It was also important whether the post was located on a territory where many Partisan units operated or if it was in the middle of Home Defense territory. Smaller units were also needed to protect the industry. This was the case in Bobovk, or at a hospital in Golnik. The last posts were also founded closer to the border as instructed. That was the case with the Kokra post.

The new post was set up when the locals asked for it and if the headquarters considered a certain post would be of great importance for the whole formation, for propaganda reasons, and the territory they were able to control would increase their area of control while still easy enough to defend. In some cases the Home Defense moved from territories and locations because they believed it was too dangerous to stay and they felt threatened. So the post in Lesce

---

[30] Archive of Republic Slovenia, Office II, former archive with the Institute for Modern History, fund Slovensko domobranstvo, fasc. Gorenjsko domobranstvo I/1.

moved to Brezje and the men from the post Ribno moved to Zagorica. When a man joined the post, SS-Oberscharfuehrer Dichtl asked the labor office to exempt the man from labor service. The workers who worked in the factories which produced war material for the army and also those who worked on the Loibl tunnel, which connected Slovenia to Carinthia through a tunnel in the Karawanken Alps, could not get an allowance from the office and thus could not legally join the Home Defense.

By the end of 1943 465 individuals had already joined the Carnolian Home Defense. Those were the men from the western posts located near the border with the Ljubljana Province and the Carnolians who had already joined the Slovene Home Guard and then came to join the Gorenjsko domobranstvo. In the next year at least four times as many men joined the Gorenjsko domobranstvo. In November 1944 over 300 men joined the formation alone. Almost the same number of men joined the following month, in December when 271 men joined. A considerable register is seen also in January 1945 – when over 400 men joined the posts. As the end of war was approaching, the average number of recruits each month was still around 200 men!

The months of March and April, 1944 are characteristic because the new posts in Škofja Loka and Kranj were founded and a lot of men who were threatened by the Partisans and those who hid, came to the post and sought protection. The men joined the Gorenjsko domobranstvo also in the last months of war, in April and May, 1945. Those were mainly juvenile men who just put on the Home Defense uniforms when they left for Carinthia with their older brothers and fathers. At post in Črni Vrh was very active in the first months of 1944. In January 43 men joined, and in March another 39 came in. The post in Škofja Loka was founded by 52 men. In August, 1944 54 men joined the Domžale post, while in January, 1945, another 90 men were accepted. In the statistical records of the home guard actions between November 25th, 1944 to January 10th, 1945 it is seen that 132 Partisans surrendered, and 211 volunteers joined the Home Defense.

Three-hundred-sixty men were forcibly mobilized into the German Army in Upper Carnolia, that is Slovenians who had previously served as German soldiers, and had later joined the Home Defense. They represented 10% of all the members in the posts. There were **more former Partisans** - 28% at the posts of the Home Defense than former German Army men. It is interesting to note that nearly all German Army deserters who later joined the Gorenjsko domobranstvo stayed for some time with the Partisans and then decided to desert from the Partisan units as well. The men who were forcibly mobilized into the German army or were German army deserters stayed in the German army from between one month to a year and a half. The ex-German Army Slovenian soldiers who joined the *domobranci* were territorialy born in the area of the Brezje River Sava River and Kamniška Bistririca.

The majority of former German soldiers came to the Home Defense posts in the second half of 1944. Some individuals hid after they returned home from the Eastern Front. Up to twenty of them hid before they joined Partisans and 10 of them hid also after deserting from Partisan units. There are some cases when a man was hiding for two years before he joined the *domobranci*. The recruitment of Slovenian manpower was severe. They were mobilized by the *domobranci* or the Partisans who would come to their homes and take them to them by force either to training camps in the cities (for the *domobranci*), or the forests (for the Partisans).

When more posts were raised the recruitment of Slovenian men who served as former German soldiers increased. The Home Defence leadership began to find out whether there were some men who would like to join *domobranci*. Dichtl arranged everything with the *Gestapo* that every man could get a furlough in Klagenfurt men already waited for him and took him with to Gorenjska and later it was reported to his unit that he deserted to Partisans. So with the help of the *Selbstschutz* and the *Marschbefehl* (marching orders) they succeeded in aiding at least 200 deserters from the German army[31]. That was quite contrary to the experience of the Kranj Home Defense post where the *Gestapo* came to arrest the ex-German Army soldiers serving in the *domobranci*.

The German units sent letters of inquiry to the districts where the men lived. In the letters usually followed the reasons for desertion, the list of relatives and a notice to the nearest *Gendarmerie* post. Nearly all former German Army soldiers who joined the *domobranci* were initially with a Partisan unit. The majority stayed only fourteen days with the Partisans and then deserted again. The post from Brezje had the most former German soldiers: about 45% of this post was made up of German Army veterans. This was the case probably because the soldiers were only allowed to come on furlough to Klagenfurt, Austria, and Brezje was the northernmost post closest to Klagenfurt, when travelling by rail from Austria. The posts of Goričane, Kovor, and Predoslje had more then 20% ex-German soldiers. The posts of Kovor, Domžale, Škofja Loka and Žabnica had the most ex-Partisan deserters.

---

[31] Archive of Republic Slovenia, Office III, former archive with Ministry of Internal Affairs, Šmajd's archive.

There were almost no former Slovenian ex-German Army soldiers in the villages around Škofja Loka. In all only ten former veterans were stationed in these posts. It is interesting to note that the posts of Črni Vrh, Gorenja vas, and Lučine did not have any former German soldiers. In fact the posts in Gorenja vas and Lučine did not have any Partisan deserters as well. Those posts belonged to the Customs Guards *(Grenze-Wache)*. We can understand that the territory was under the strong influence of the Home Defence posts of the *Slovensko domobranstvo* and the Germans controlled the four posts of Carnolia Home Defense. So even though the men were born in that area, they would rather go to the posts at Šent Jošt or Rovte.

The fear that they would be caught and sent back to the German front was very much present. In the Assault Company more then half of the men were either former Partisans or ex-German Army veterans. Even the Partisan reports admitted that desertions were a very common event. They reported that four Partisan political commanders for and two battalion commanders had deserted for political reasons and had gone over to the *domobranci* post at Goričane.

Former German Army soldiers were very welcomed at the posts because they could handle weapons, and they were skilled fighters and were younger. The Slovenian [German Army] veterans on leave stayed mostly in a hotel in Laznik Street, in Klagenfurt. Both, the Partisans and *domobranci* would come there and many times tried to persuade them to join their formations. The majority of these Slovenian veterans had been wounded at the front. Sometimes they even shot themselves in order to be repatriated, and had received sick leave. They knew that they would have little chance to survive if they returned to their [German] units. Almost all of them wanted to return home and not to fight for the Germans.

The Home Defense referred to the Partisans as *"gošar"* (forest men), "bandits," "communists," or "OF-bandits" (Liberation Front bandits). When former Partisans joined the *domobranci* posts, the leaders were very indulgent: *"When the news spread that a new post of the Home Defence was founded, a large group of volunteers would come. Those were mostly former Partisans, who joined the Partisan movement because they believed that they were fighting for the freedom of their nation. But they soon found out that the bandits did not care for the welfare of the nation and that they were nothing more than followers of the Communist International which, in the eyes of many, had sold out the fatherland."*[32]

On September 15th, 1944 the time limit for the Partisan amnesty ran out. Only a few deserters reported in. In the Škofja Loka district there

---

[32] Karawanken Bote, 4. 11. 1944

were over 700 homes belonging to families of the Home Defense, but only three men from there reported to the Partisan units. Nevertheless, in September 1944 a drop in recruitment was seen at the *domobranci* posts. Probably the reason was due to an increase in Partisan propaganda.

During the second Partisan amnesty, which lasted until January 15th, 1945, it was quite the opposite. In that month alone, more than 400 men joined the *domobranci* posts! What is so amazing is that by then, the war was nearly at the end and the Germans were clearly seen as the losers! How could this phenomena be explained? It could have been perhaps because it was in the middle of the winter which was always the worst time for guerrilla units, and the German offensive against the Partisans which was going on at that time. Perhaps it was also that the average man did not have enough information on the events in the European fronts and could therefore not understand clearly that the Germans were losing the war.

The Partisans tried to counter this by using propaganda tools on a large scale. They scattered leaflets which said: *"To the Home Defense! If you do not rob, burn, or kill you will be in good graces with us. Take the benevolence of our government, otherwise your head will fall. The hours you have spent will not come back. Do you wish the January 15th deadline to suck you into the maelstrom"* Also ex-Ministers of the former Yugoslav government, among them Minister Kuhar, who were in London, also appealed to the *domobranci* to forsake the Germans and join the Partisans. The intellectuals who left and traveled abroad, Mr. Izidor Cankar, and Dr. Furlan, joined in the appeal. The Yugoslav King Peter IInd also called on the *domobranci* to desert as well.

On the other hand, the newspapers of the Home Defense stimulated the men to join the posts and quoted: *"The January 15th is over. To all those who were ensnared and did not spill their brothers' blood, our doors are open. It is the final time to cast off that sulky companionship."* In the poems they wrote: The poem for January 15th 1945: *"Oh, the charm of poetry, oh the charm of the words, oh the charm of the fifteenth, oh charm of amnesty. You didn't get anyone into your clutches, into your mare's nest, the lady amnesty"*[33].

The Partisan deserters came to the Home Defence posts during all of these months, but the majority registered in <u>January 1945</u>. After joining the post a man was under continuous control by his the immediate NCO, who was usually a corporal, plus an informant and the post commander until he proved by his acts, deeds, and private life and relation with their colleagues that he could be trusted.

---

[33] Gorenjski domobranec, January 1945.

The *Gorenjsko domobranstvo* accepted mainly only volunteers, but after interrogation of captured Partisan prisoners, they accepted also deserters from other formations. In the post at Brezje they reported:

"...all the arrested who are interrogated and seem to be sincere are made to stay for some days in the posts in order to see life on the post and to hear about the Home Defense and its principles. Then they are sent home. They agree that the attitude toward the newcomers should be appealing"[34]. The *domobranci* also printed and distributed propaganda notices: *"In the fight against communism, no one should be exempt, even you Upper Carnolians, death to bolshevism, forward with Adolf Hitler!"*

The Center [Headquarters] of the *Gorensko domobranstvo* sent a letter to the commanders of all posts, requesting them to make a list of those men who were, either because of age or due to illness, not capable of military actions. This list was also to include the names of defeatists and alarmists, and all others who might cause trouble. The procedure as to how to treat a captured Partisan was written down in the regulation book. The commander and informer made a record of the interrogation, it was read back to the interrogated prisoner, and the former Partisan was asked to sign it. The commander and informer were now also required to sign the document. It was strictly ordered that an interrogation as to be carried out as soon as the former Partisan arrived at the post. Then the commander was obliged to send the captive to the Center Headquarters. The ones who could not be accepted into the ranks of the *Gorenjsko domobranstvo*, were sent to the *Gestapo Aussenstelle*. The *domo-branstvo* registered the volunteers for whom there was no doubt that they were anticommunist oriented. The senior Home Defensemen were then asked to try to influence the newcomers.

Partisan notices reported that some men also deserted from the *domobranstvo* to Partisans. In March, 1944 30 men deserted from the posts in Gorenja vas, and some from Črni Vrh. Sometimes this occurred for family or personal reasons, as the members of the posts were exchanged. They were transferred with all their equippment - caps, blouses, trousers, underwear, tableware, tent cloth, belt, a pair of socks, shoes, gloves, their weapon and ammunition, and some hand grenades. This happened especially as the end of war was approaching and the list or the register of the men at the post was not always accurate.

---

[34] Archive of Republic Slovenia, Office II, fund Slovensko domobranstvo, Gorenjsko domobranstvo, Reports to the Center, December 1944.

Center [Headquarters] of the Gorenjsko domobranstvo

On November 6th, 1944 the Center Headquarters of the *Gorenjsko domobranstvo* was established. The official report was dated as December 4th, 1944. The appointed leader of the Center was Slavko Krek. In the beginning of November, 1944 the instructors from Ljubljana came to introduce their brand of Home Guard military discipline, and to train the men and to strengthen their hold over these men by establishing this "Central Headquarters of the *Gorenjsko domobranstvo*." They came dressed in the uniforms of the *Slovensko domobranstvo* and were sent to the posts in Suhi Dol, Litija, Domžale, Cerklje, Mengeš, Goričane, Kovor, Lahoviče, Črni Vrh and Lesce - altogether 29 of them. These men were members of the Slovene League and Falcon League. Since the *Slovensko domobranstvo* were not allowed for to collaborate with the *Gorenjsko domobranstvo* they were led in the register under fictitious names. They were very successful and some of them later became commanding officers of some posts.

In the autumn of 1944 new additional ranks were introduced. The posts received, besides a commander and a deputy commander, a *"vodnik"* and propaganda men. In addition, the Center Headquarters also appointed lance corporals, instructors and informers. The corporals were appointed by the Center, it was the same with propagandist and informers, but only the commander of the post could make a recommendation for their nomination. The instructors were appointed on the recommendation of the Commander of the *Gorenjsko domobranstvo*, which was *SS-Oberscharfuehrer* Erich Dichtl. Since January 1st, 1945 the posts, except for posts which belonged to the customs guards, were directly supplied from the Center Headquarters. The hierarchical pyramid looked as followed. On top was the commander of the SIPO and SD at Bled (Veldes), *SS-Obersturmbannfuehrer* Alois Poersterer, then immediately below was the commander of the *Gorenjsko domobranstvo*, Erich Dichtl who was a member of the *Gestapo Aussenstelle* Kranj[35].

The Chief Political Commissar was *SS-Obersturmfuehrer* Rudolf Messner, who was the commander of the Gestapo Aussenstelle in Kranj. The Commander of the Center Headquarters of the *Gorenjsko domobranstvo* was as already stated, Slavko Krek. The officer in charge of Military Discipline was Marjan Fludernik, while the head of the Intelligence Service was Janez Ovsenik. The head of the Propaganda Department was Alojz Perne, while the Commander in

---

[35] Gestapo Branch Office in Krainburg.

Chief for Police Activity was Milan Amon. Each post had two orderlies and one of them was a sort of representative of the post at Center. Besides daily and weekly reports, the posts had to send to the SIPO as well as the Center Headquarters, the list of wounded and dead, and the number of Partisan captives and deserters.

The proclamation which created the Headquarters Center of the *Gorenjsko domobranstvo* clearly stated that the men of the *Gorenjsko domobranstvo* wanted to be led by the SIPO and that they were subordinated to this organization in regards to disciplinary, supply, and all other military matters. The men at the posts could carry out their own actions only if the order was given by the *Gestapo Aussenstelle* or if they had an officer in charge from the *Gestapo*. They could arrest or confiscate and ransack dwellings only in accordance with *Gestapo* directives. The commander of the Central Headquarters was answerable to Dichtl and Messner. His reports had to go to them. Krek had weekly meetings with the district leader of NSDAP Dr. Walter Hochsteiner, and they discussed the relation of the *Gorenjsko domobranstvo* with German authorities.

In contrast to the Slovene Home Guard, the *Gorenjsko domobranstvo* did not take the oath of allegiance. A Partisan source stated that the Home Defense oath was to be administered on April 15th, 1945 but that would probably have been the oath for the members of the "Slovene National Army, and this oath was never really carried out. Many men complained to Krek that their commanders did not allow the ex-German Army Slovene veterans to wear German badges and medals. Krek ordered that they had to wear them. The only problem was that nobody could really know if indeed the badges were really won while in the service of the *Wehrmacht*,[36] or while in the *domobranci* because the badges were the same. So the *domobranci* were awarded the decorations which were actually German decorations: the Wound Badge, War Merit Cross, 2nd class with Swords and a the Bravery Badge, although there are no reports indicating that anyone in the Upper Carnolia Home Defense Force ever received the Bravery Badge.

On September 10th, 1944 seven Home Defensemen were awarded the wound badge. On that occasion units of the *Gorenjsko domo-branstvo* marched through Kranj with Erich Dichtl at its head. The *Kreisleiter* (Area Leader) of the NSDAP, Hochsteiner was also present and Posthumously awarded Rudolf Humer from Škofja Loka with the War Merit Cross, 2nd Class, with Swords. In January, 1945 1st Lieutenant Franc Erpič also received the War Merit Cross. He was awarded the badge for attacking the Headquarters of the Partisan

---

[36] *Wehrmacht-* German Armed Forces (all branches).

"Prešern" Brigade, together with ten *domobranci,* and also for saving a sister of the Home Guard who was in danger of being killed[37].

The *Gauleiter* (District Leader) of Carinthia, Dr Alois Friedrich Rainer stated in his speech in December, 1944 that he would not change anything in the organisation of the *Gorenjsko domobranstvo,* especially in the *Slovensko domobranstvo,* as the latter organization hoped that he would incorporate them together with the former[38]. He said that the main interest of the Germans was to have the Home Defense to help protect them from the Partisan menace. The commander, *SS-Oberscharfuehrer* Erich Dichtl wrote to the *Arbeitsamt* (Labor Office) in Klagenfurt in October, 1944 and stated that it was important to strengthen the *Gorenjsko domobranstvo,* because the men serving in this force protected the heavy industry and the lives of the German people in Upper Carnolia.

He also said that everyday they were losing more men, and because of the war, hundreds and hundreds of men from Upper Carnolia were either mobilized or were needed in other capacities outside the homeland. He then requested that the Labor Office recall at least a smaller number of men from work in Germany in order to incorporate them into the units which were fighting against the Partisans. The *Gendarmerie* detachments received a special report to take care that they would not equate the *Gorenjska Home Defense* with the *Slovensko Home Guard* because in Upper Carnolia there were only *Gorenjska* Home Defense men. In other words, Dichtl was warning the German frontier police to leave the Upper Krajina Slovenian troops alone.

Walter Hochsteiner, the leader of the NSDAP[39] in the Kranj District, deposed at his trial after the war, that after the capitulation of Italy the situation got worse and by then the Germans considered raising independent self-defense units[40]. The Home Defensemen did not trust the German police, and neither did the Germans completely trust the *domobranci*[41]. Generally speaking, the mood at the post

---

[37] Written statement, F.E.

[38] The Home Defense of the Ljubljana Province with the Home Defense of the Gorenjsko Home Defense

[39] NSDAP- Abbreviation for German National Socialist Workers Party.

[40] Gorenjski muzej, Kranj, fund trial Hochsteiner.

[41] A perfect example was the disarming of the Home Defense post at Bistrica, by the SS on December 30th, 1944. The German report, which was dated "14 January, 1945" was found in NARS microfilm document Series T-501, Roll 261, Frame 000547. It originally surfaced and appeared on page 65 of

was anti-German although from some posts declared that they would stand with the Germans. On average there were no German units stationed together in the Home Defense posts. At the posts which belonged to the *Grenzpolizei* (Frontier Police) German border guards and German Police could be found, but no *domobranci*. It was the same in the Škofja Loka post, but the posts in the Kranj District were rarely visited by the Germans. Sometimes *SS-Oberscharfuehrer* Erich Dichtl would come by a post that had recently been engaged, in order to check up on the situation.

The Home Defense made many appeals to the Germans asking them to spare the villages near the border with Carinthia, and that the homes should not be burnt down, citing that many families living in that frontier region had their sons in German Army, and were in this way showing loyalty to the Germans, so for that reason alone their homes should be spared. General Leon Rupnik mentioned this at his trial in 1946, stating that Roesener tried to form an SS division of men from Upper Krajina (Gorenjska) and Styria (Štajerska). But that he (Rupnik) had dissuaded the SS General from this scheme because he believed that the majority of the Home Defense men intended for this Slovenian SS division, would flee to the forests that is- to the Partisans at the slightest opportunity.

Krek had weekly meetings with the head of *Reichspropagandaamt*-the Nazi Propaganda Office in Bled. He was also constantly travelling to Ljubljana (Laibach) and often brought information to Mirko Bitenc. The posts which were answerable to the border guards usually had communications with the posts of the *Slovensko domobranstvo* every two weeks. On the posts in Domžale and Litija orderlies of the "Melacher" Chetnik Group from Styria often stopped by. In February, 1945 the *Gestapo* arrested some Home Defensemen and accused them of not being enough pro-German. They discovered some documents proving that the *domobranci* had tried to establish contacts with the western Allies. Some men who were linked to this "plot" were also arrested in Ljubljana, and sent to the Dachau concentration camp. The men were mostly the members of Slovene League. On February 28th, 1945 the *Gestapo* arrested five Home Defense men, while some who were still being hunted, went underground and in that way escaped being arrested.

The Home Guard in Gorenjska did not come into contact with the western Allies, although the men at these northern posts believed in common cause with the western Allies. It was also important that in the posts which were under Chetnik influence this belief was stronger.

"Slovenian Axis Forces in World War II, 1941-1945" by Antonio J. Munoz. Axis Europa Books: Bayside, NY 1997.

Those were mainly posts located in Predoslje and Cerklje. In January, 1945 the Home Defense men from Gorenja vas received Allied supplies which were meant for the Partisans. On January 15th, 1945 Allied planes dropped two parcels in blue and red colored packages[42]. The Home Defense men who intercepted these parcels received 5 mortars, some clotheing and other small arms for their trouble.

From October 15th to 22nd, 1944 a group of Chetniks bivouacked in the village Predoslje. They were accompanied by a group of rescued Allied airmen. U.S. Army Air Corps pilot William Ludwig was one of them. His nickname was Stric-Uncle, because at the farm where he was hiding, the family told everyone that their uncle from America had arrived. So Ludwig was not suspicious. At various times the Gorenjska Chetnik Detachment also had 15 other Allied airmen in their care. From testemonies it is seen that they were all handed over to the Germans. In February, 1945 an attempt on the life of Slavko Krek was carried out. He was wounded and had to be hospitalized in Ljubljana. The *Gestapo* came there to arrest him but he escaped and fled to Gorenjska. For some time he also stayed with the Chetnik Headquarters in Polhograjski Dolomiti.

An attempt on the life of Erich Dichtl was carried out in March, 1945. Dichtl was not only in charge of the *Gorenjska domobranstvo,* but was the Commander of the Kranj Home Defense post. He and his chauffer, plus an interpreter left the Home Guard post in Radovljica and after about ten kilometers they fell into a Partisan ambush. The driver and the interpreter were killed, while Dichtl escaped with minor scratches. In December, 1944 the Center Headquarters sent rubber stamps to the commanders of every posts. Now every report that a post sent to Center Headquarters had to be stamped in the upper left corner of the document with the rubber imprint of the post.

In March, 1945 the commander of the SIPO and SD requested that the rubber stamps be turned over to his command in Kranj in order to invalidate them. That move signalled the official end of Center Headquarters of the *Gorenjsko domobranstvo.* The staff moved with the Kranj post to Stražišče. Krek was hiding underground, his men from the Headquarters were arrested, and Ovsenik was sent to the branch of Mauthausen Concentration Camp at the Loibl Tunnel. The Headquarters Center still operated until the end of war, but it was not organized in the same manner as it had been before and the name was changed. It was no longer referred to as the "Center," but simply the Headquarters of the *Gorenjsko domobranstvo.* The remaining

---

[42] The Slovenian national colors are White, Blue, and Red.

officers prepared and signed the documents which were sent to the posts.

The first organizers of the new Center Headquarters, were Milan Amon and Franc Šenk who initially led the organization. In January, 1945 Senk and Amon organized a Home Guard Officer's Course at Brdo near Kranj. The castle and the estate belonged before the war to the Royal Karadjordjević Family. Each time the course was given, more than 100 men attended. The Head Instructor of the courses was Franc Rigler, a Slovene Home Guard officer who came to Brdo from the post at Dravlje, which was located near the border in Ljubljana. Ernest Hirschegger now led the Intelligence Service and Technical Organization. Jože Vidmar, Dane Hribar and the Jože and Nikolaj Žužek brothers gave lectures. The themes were on ideological problems introduced by Slavko Krek, Maks Jan, Janez Ovsenik and Franc Pernišek.

The men were not very enthusiastic about going to the courses because a rumor had spread stating that the men would then be sent to the front after the end of courses. The 1st School Company, which consisted of commanders of different posts who had come to attend the course, was founded at Brdo on January 9th, 1945. The first course continued for a month. On February 20th, 1945 the 2nd Course began- this one for NCO's[43]. Home Defense men had to bring to the course their weapon, a blanket, a straw mattress, tableware, suffucient under-wear, uniforms, shoes, shaving gear, and a toothbrush for three weeks, plus a notebook. Only the best men were sent to take these courses. The posts had to give them their daily ration cards (coupon book) for food, cigarettes, soap, and salary.

Partisan reports wrote that about 500 Home Guardsmen were sent to the front, but in fact, only some 50 men went to Tržič, about 20 km from Kranj and organized a new post. After the men returned to their posts, the leaders of the course sent them letters in which they wanted to know whether they kept order, and if they had learned anything at the courses which had allowed them additional information on how to organize the life on the posts.

Daily Life on a Typical Post

The organization daily life at the Home Guard posts was quite unique. During the day, there weren't too many men present at the posts, only the ones who were on duty. The men from the posts worked at home, on their farms and so nearly every day left the post and went home. Quite often they worked in the field with a gun over

---

[43] Specifically, for corporals.

their shoulder, and they returned to the posts only to spend the night there. The majority of the members of the Home Defense had farms and in addition to their Home Guard duties, a lot of work awaited them in their homes. Also the Home Defense leadership agreed that the domestic work should go on without any delays. Thus, we can say that the Home Defense men were tied down to their farms.

The men from the post in Kranj could not go home everyday day. Because of the distance, they could only go home if they asked for one or two days leave. Discipline was much stricter in the Kranj Post, and the men had to obey the regulations. On the regular posts, an entire support service was organzied – There was the head of the Home Defense office, Head of the (local) Inteligence Service, Head and Deputy of the Criminal Department, Clerical Employee, Propagandist, two Orderlies, an Armorer, Cook, Shoemaker, Tailor, and Hospital Orderly. A typical day in the life of a Home Defense post looked very much like the one at the post in Smlednik. They would awake at 5 a.m., after the morning report the majority of the men went home, only the ones who were on duty that day remained at the post, and in the evening all the men returned to the post for the night.

At the Predoslje post, the men attended a class on discipline from 9 to 10 a.m., and from 2 to 4 p.m. the post would launch patrols. From 5 to 6 p.m. various, different duties would take up their time. The 8th item of report stating founding of the Center Headquarters of the Upper Carnolia Home Defense force described the uniforms which they used. The men were given grey-green uniforms as used by the SIPO and SD. The jacket was lacking the normal piping. The trousers were long and "pointed." The spiked mountain shoes were worn, as well as the peaked mountain cap with the German national eagle on the left side in cloth. For their national emblem, they wore a shield with the Slovenian singleheaded eagle in blue and a blue-red background. This cloth emblemt was worn on the left sleeve. The men of the Assault Company also wore the Death's Head skull insignia on the left collar tab.

For rank insignia, the Commander of Cener Headquarters wore three gold braids 10 cm long and 1.5 cm wide- one from each other on the edge of the right sleeve. The heads of each particular service, such as intelligence, propaganda, police etc., wore two gold braids, while their deputies wore one gold braid. The commanders of the posts wore three silver braids 10 cm long 1.5 cm wide one from each other.

A Lance-Sergeant (vodnik) wore two silver braids, a Lance-Corporal (desetnik) wore only one. Home Defense men had to sew the national cloth emblem on the left sleeve of the jacket 15 cm under the seam of the sleeve. It was forbidden to forge, trim or colour the emblem. Although it was regulated what a uniform of a Gorenjska Home Defenseman should be, the Home Defense uniforms differed. They all wore jackets and trousers. At some posts their tailors made uniforms of the camouflage material which the allies sent to the Partisans and Home Defense units seized this camouflage cloth. They also wore different cockades. From the Krajina Eagle, to an oval tricolour with an eagle, much like the Slovenski domobranstvo.

At the post in Smlednik they wore a tricolour strip which they tied between the buttons on the cap. The Home Defense men could wear their own shirts and cravattes. Some Home Defense men had an additional uniform. The men washed the underwear at home. But not all Home Defense men had a uniform. Those who did not have a uniform were sent to Kranj to the Center Headquarters. At the posts there were also some civilians, although they were registred as Home Defense men. They were usually shoemakers, cooks or other craftsmen. Former deserters from the German Army did not get a new uniform, they only put on the Home Defense emblem. If a Home Defense man was killed, he was not buried in a uniform, but in a civilian clothes. This was done for the obvious sake of preserving uniforms for the next volunteer.

When the Home Defense withdrew to Carinthia some of them took along civilian clothes with them. Some saved their lives with them. Many times the Partisans appeared and blocked a column which was withdrawing towards Carinthia and demanded that the Home Defense men remove their emblems. At the beginning of the withdrawal, some Home Defense men had the presense of mind to put on a Šajkača (former Yugoslav soft cover) because in May, 1945 it was announced that the Gorenjsko domobranstvo was now a part of the Slovene National Army. The British soldiers would allow the Chetniks through their lines, and they also were not forced to turn in their weapons. All they needed was an utterance he was a Chetnik and that person would be let through without hindrance. Later, a thesis was formed about the German Sipo/SD police uniform. Someone rightly judged that this SS uniform was fatal for the destiny of the men.

When Home Defensemen were handed over to Tito's forces, the shoes and other parts of the uniform which were in good condition were very often seized by the Partisans. The ones who returned home safely had to bring in their uniform to Partisan district headquarters. Some men burned their uniforms as soon as they came home, while some simply dyed the wool to some other color. This was done because immediately after the war there was a real need for clothing and good material was hard to come by. The Home Defense men saluted with a typical military salute. The so-called Hitler salute, with outstretched hand, was never introduced to the

Home Defense in Gorenjska for political reasons. Each month the post had to make a lists of all the Home Defense men. Their names had to be written in the German language although later, a separate, secondary list in Slovenian was introduced for each post.

The commanders of the posts gave orders in the Slovene language, but the Home Defense men had to be familiar with the German language and basic German commands. Many lived already in the Austro-Hungarian monarchy, and had survived the Great War in the Austro-Hungarian Army. In addition, because of the border with Austria, Slovenians had always pursued learning the German language. They also had to know German commands because they would sometimes go into action led by officers and NCO's of the Gestapo.

The Home Defense men earned 5 *Reichmarks* daily, and whenever they went into battle, they received 10 *RM*. On the fifth of every month the payment register was sent to the local Gestapo Aussensetlle. But the salaries came only now and then, and in the last months of the war, they even did not arrive at all. It mostly depended on the commander of the post whether the men got their salaries or not. In the last months of war the commanders were reported to have received 700 *RM* per month. The Germans also paid a family allowance, about 30-40 *RM* per child. The posts which belonged to the Frontier Guard were paid from the Ministry of Finance.

The posts which were located in the mountains received their supplies from the posts which were located down in the valleys. They brought the supplies mostly by carts or on horseback. The orderlies had bicycles and some even possessed cars, but in the winter months they used sleighs. Cleanliness was always a problem. At the post in Škofja Loka they reported that because of unsanitary conditions, lice had appeared. The units also had to do obligatory bathing, as well as medical and dental checkups. Some of the men of the Home Defense had very bad teeth. The Home Defense men from smaller posts were supplied food and weapons from larger posts. In some smaller posts they even did not cook at all, and the men were directed to eat at the nearest private home. The posts received ration cards (actually coupon books) for oil, pepper, cinnamon, and paprika. The men desired great amounts of margarine and marmalade, which were used in the everyday eating.

The cooks were usually the wives or sisters of the men from the post, or women who deserted from the Partisan movement. Discipline was another problem. The Partisans reported that in some Home Defense posts the Gestapo men guarded the post. The Slovenian Home Guard in Lučine and Črni Vrh were pro-German in their orientation, and believed that the Germans would take them under their protection if they were forced to withdraw from Gorenjska. In Cerklje the Home Guardsmen were hoping that the western Allies would come. The discipline in these posts was problematic. They reported that the men divided themselves into " Home Guards" and "self guards". The Home Defense men who were punished were sent to prisons at their posts, but for larger offenses they were sent to Brdo Castle. The men who were demoralized or did not believe in a Home Defense movement or victory, were sent to take a course to Brdo, although it was said that only the best shoud go to Brdo. Some Home Defense men were arrested and sent to prisons in Begunje.

In March 1945, a Home Defenseman was brought up on charges and accused of being an English spy. He was sent to the Loibl Camp, a branch of Mauthausen Concentration Camp. Some men were brought to Begunje because of connections with the Partisans. Begunje prison was the biggest prison in Gorenjska. Mainly Partisans who were caught and their families were imprisoned there. A lot of hostages who were shot at different places in Gorenjska were brought from that prison and about 30 prisoners were sent to the Home Defense post in Brezje. Those were mainly Partisan deserters. Even in April, 1945 the *Gestapo Aussenstelle* received an order that they should not sent the captured Partisans to the Begunje prisons but to the Home Defense posts.

For larger offenses, the men could be discharged from the formation. Some were dismissed for being accused of collaborationg with the Partisans. One Home Defense man was shot in front of his squad for collaborating with the Partisans. During an air raid on Vače (near Litija), some Home Defense men were killed. The morale fell and the commander asked the Center to send ten Home Defense men to exchange them with the men from his post for propaganda reasons. The Assault Company, which was very efficient, was called to instill fear into the demoralized men, who admitted that the best pro-paganda was a machine gun.

Structure

The majority of the Home Defense men were born between the years of 1900 and 1910 - exactly 526 of them. The older men prevailed at the posts because the younger ones were called up for service in the German Army. A good number of the younger men deserted and joined the Home Defense. This group, born between 1920 and 1924 was numerous: 465 men. There were only a few born between 1915-1920, probably because of the First World War and one of its effects: a low birthrate. Eighty men were born before the year of 1900. Quite often there were two generations of the same family at the same posts, usually father and son(s).

The youngest man officially registered in the Gorenjsko domobranstvo was born in 1929 and was sixteen years old in 1945. The posts in Litija and Suhi Dol had younger men. The men at the post in Brezje were mostly born between 1920 to 1925. There were mostly men who deserted from the German Army and the first post on the Slovenian territory to which they registered when returning from the Eastern Front. In the Assault Company, troops who were younger in age prevailed. In the posts which belonged to the *Grenzpolizei* (Frontier Police) there were mostly older men. The first 80 Home Defense men who joined Gorenjsko domobranstvo were mostly born between 1905 and 1915.

The men enlisted at the posts in the vicinity of their homes and stayed there. The Home Defense idea involved also protecting homes and all of the Home Defense men wanted to be as near as possible to their homes. The men were mostly farmers and also factory workers, especially in the posts near the industrial centers. At the Voklo post there were 25 farmers, 4 workers, 1 painter, 1 student, a tailor, blacksmith, butcher, carpenter, and a weaver. At the Smlednik post there were 27 farmers, 33 workers and one tailor, miller, and bricklayer. More information is available on the professions of men from particular villages who joined the Home Defense. Among the first 61 men who joined the Gorenjsko domobranstvo in the spring of 1944 were 40 farmers, one miller, one blacksmith, three shoemakers, one mechanic, eleven factory workers, two carpenters, one tailor, and one student. There were not a lot of men with a university education.

One third of the men from the posts were married. At the same post was often a father and two or three sons. At the Škofja Loka post there were 30 men married who, together, had 121 children, while in Cerklje, 29 men out of 113 were married. They had 78 children. Some domobranci were married during the war. It is seen from statistical data that the birth places and the places where they married and lived during the war were very often the same. The domobranci wanted to serve at the local post. The actions between the Upper Carniola Home Defense and Partisan actions against them were mostly restricted to the region of the post. The Home Defense men did not go very often go into major actions. They mainly attended guard duty and arrested supporters of the Partisan movement, patrolled around the nearby villages and disposed of books and other literature which were considered Partisan propaganda. Slovenian lance-sergeants trained soldiers at the posts and led the groups in patrols.

The number of lance sergeants depended on the number of the men. A Domobran unit went into action only after the action was approved by the German Police / SIPO, they also arrested only with the *Gestapo's* approval and after an interrogation, they had to turn over the prisoners to the German Police. The posts operated mostly only in their territory. Only from time to time did they go to other posts on a large march or search and destroy operation.

The main actions which the Home Guard did with the *Gestapo* were: An operation in the region of Styria to Gornji Grad in December, 1944 and January 1945 (the posts at Domžale, and Tupaliče, plus the Assault Battalion took part) This was a large German offensive against the liberated territory in Styria.

A march (sweep) to Kropa in Upper Carniola in January, 1945. The posts from Kovor, Bobovek, Kranj, Lahovče, Mavčiče, Smlednik, Brezje and Tupaliče took part in this march.

A battle which took part from Idrija to Žiri in April, 1945. The posts from Škofja Loka, Žabnica, Sopotnica, Bitnje, Gorenja vas, Suhi Dol, Lučine and Črni Vrh took part. This was one of the last German offensives against Partisans.

The posts near the border with the former Ljubljana Province were very active already in the beginning of 1944. They took part in operations with the *Gendarmerie* (Rural Police) and *Grenzpolizei* (Frontier Police) posts. In one of these battles against the Partisans in April, 1944 the Home Defense men from the Lučine post had six men wounded. The *Gendarmerie* post from Gorenja vas reported that *Grenzpolizei* and Domobranci jointly operated, going to nearby villages. A post from Gorenja vas fought with Partisans over the town of Hotavlje in September, 1944. In a battle near Butajnova, the men of the Home Guard posts from Suhi Dol, Črni Vrh, Lučine and Šent Jošt all took part. With them were twenty Germans of the SD and SiPo. The Germans suffered three dead, while the Home Guard lost one dead and one wounded from the Lučine post, and one wounded from the post at Suhi Dol, while the post at Črni Vrh lost two dead, and five wounded.

The Assault Company which at this time had seventy-two men, and was under the leadership of Franc Erpič, went to Styria on December 1st 1944. At first they travelled by cars and other vehicles from Kranj to Kamnik. They were incorporated into a German police regiment[44] which fought in the region Kamnik-Gornji Grad. Partisan propaganda was very strong there. The people were afraid of the Home Defense, because it was said that *"the Home Defense men gouged out the eyes of everyone forcibly mobilised"*. In the first four days they did not

---

[44] Possibly, SS Police Regiment 25, which was operating with only one battalion (the Ist), and therefore was in need of reinforcements.

encounter any Partisans. On December 19th, 1944 they had some battles with the Partisans and killed six of them.

They captured a female Partisan fighter and took one light machine gun, one English machine pistol, one horse and three field glasses. On December 8th, 1944 the Home Defense came to the hospital at Podvolovjek. In their reports they quote that they killed two Partisans and arrested nine of them. They said that they had left 12 heavily wounded Partisans in the hospital. In the Partisan reports it was quoted that the Home Defense men followed the "Zidanšek" Partisan Brigade and discovered a Partisan hospital where 114 partisans lay wounded. Together with the Germans, the Home Defense men killed 30 wounded Partisans at the hospital. 16 captured Partisans were handed over to the Germans who killed them at Ljubno and 6 were hanged in Frankolovo. As we can see, the events differ greatly, depending on who is telling the story[45].

In the beginning of 1945 the men from the Kovor, Brezje and Mavčiče posts were sent to Kropa. A lot of snow had fallen, and there was a lot more falling at the time. Over beautiful but exhausting virgin snow, often knee deep, the Home Guard men waded through the snow. It was so cold that the machine guns could not operate. The Home Defense were accompanied by a unit of the Ukrainian 14th SS Division. On March 17th 120 men were sent to the territory of Litija. In that group were men from the Bitnje, Stražišče and Žabnica post. The Home Defense mainly had minor engagements with the Partisans. The Upper Carnolia Chetnik Detachment also took part in actions against the guerrillas late in the Fall of 1944. A commander of the Home Guard from Dravlje near Ljubljana, Milko Pirih, joined the Chetniks in June 1944. He took with him many Home Guard troops and organized the Upper Carnolia Chetnik Detachment.

They were joined by many Slovenes who were ex-German Army veterans, and had been too afraid to join the Home Defense posts. In August, 1944 this Slovene Chetnik detachment moved along the flat territories of Gorenjska and in September it merged with the Chetniks of the Lower Carnolia Chetnik Detachment and moved to Žiri, near the former border with the Ljubljana Province, some 50km west of Ljubljana. Partisans attacked them and twelve men were killed, the wounded Chetniks got medical treatment in the hospitals in Ljubljana. The Partisans also had many dead from this engagement. When the Partisans attacked a post of the Slovene Littoral Home Guard (SNVZ) at Črni Vrh near Idrija in the last days of August 1944, the Chetniks hurried to help them, but arrived too late. The Partisans had

---

[45] It is extremely difficult to write an objective history. In many cases written history is, because of our own human fallacy, subjective.- the Editor.

already demolished the post. On the September 1st, 1944 the post surrendered.

In October, 1944 the Gorenjska Chetnik Detachment went on a propaganda march to Gorenjska[46]. They were accompanied by the Dolenjska Chetnik Detachment. The action was led by Major Mirko Bitenc. They also planned a mobilisation of the men and formation of the liberated territory under the Krvavec mountain range, 30km from Kranj. On October 4th, 1944 they forded the river near Ljubljana and went to Zalog near Cerklje. The partisans attacked a public house in Srednji Zalog where the Chetniks and Home Defense were staying. Ten Chetniks were killed, among them was the new commander Franc Jerebič and *curate* Lojze Duhovnik. In the same night the Partisans attacked the Home Defense post in Lahoviče but the Gorenjska Chetnik Detachment helped the post to beat off the attack. At that time there were also some Chetniks at the post.

The Lower Carnolia Chetnik Detachment which was also present in Gorenjska did not take part in that attack. Bitenc and his men spent some weeks at the Home Defense posts. The Germans encircled the Chetniks in Predoslje and the commanders were sent to Kranj to speak with the German officers. They established for them a territory in the village Suha near Predoslje. In one house in Predoslje the Chetniks had their headquarters and also published a newspaper called *"Triglav,"* As already stated, the Chetniks had an American airmen, named William Ludwig Stric with them. The Chetnik Detachment numbered 70 men[47]. In October, 1944 quite a number of formerly conscripted ex-German Army Slovenes joined them. The Chetniks sent their men to different Home Defense posts, the majority stayed at Cerklje, Lahoviče and Kovor.

Ten Chetniks presented a group. They moved from one post to another and informed their men at the posts and gave them tasks as to what to do and how to act and collaborate with the Home Defense. The group was led by Janez Borštnar. He was later killed while crossing the border into the Ljubljana Province. The Chetniks apparently received their food, equipment, and shoes from German warehouses. The material was actually prepared for the Home Defense but they gave it to the Chetniks. In battle, the Chetniks collaborated with the Home Defense against Partisans. At the end of 1944, the smaller group of Chetniks left Predoslje, and passed Škofja Loka and came to a Chetnik base southeast of the post at Sv Jošt.

---

[46] Probably to recruit more volunteers.- the Editor.

[47] In terms of western military strengths, equivalent to a reinforced platoon or very weak company.

The other men stayed at the Gorenjska Home Defense posts. For Christmas, 1944 the Chetnik headquarters came back to Lahovče. Major Bitenc also came. In February, 1945 the *Gestapo* seized much material which belonged to the Chetniks in the houses at Predoslje. In February and March, 1945 the Chetniks went into action together with the Home Defense. At the end of April, 1945 the Chetniks attacked the Loibl Concentration Camp, near the Loibl Tunnel close to the Austrian border. The camp was a branch of Mauthausen Concentration Camp. They released one of the Home Defense organisers who was also collaborating with Chetniks. Afterwards they withdrew back to the post at Kovor.

Partisan Attacks on the Home Defense Posts

On the June 15[th,] 1944 a Home Defense post in Hotavlje was founded. It was very well fortified. Eighty-five members of the post were billeted in two houses, Nr.58 and 59 near the road. In the hill over the house was a bunker and trenches lay all around. The post was surrounded with concertina wire. The Hotavlje post was situated only a few kilometers from the post in Gorenja vas. The 31st Partisan Division, together with the "Kosovel" and some units of the "Gregorčič" and "Bazoviška" Brigade attacked the post. Simultaneously, the Partisans blocked access to and from the posts in Gorenja was and Lučine. The Partisans employed for the first time a new weapon, called a *"peartop"*, which was a locally manufactured mortar, made in the Partisan workshops. But these mortars blew up after firing their first shot. Between July 18th-19th,1944 the Home Defense repelled the large Partisan attack, but the next day the Partisans succeeded to punch a hole through a section of the fence. The majority of the Home Defense men withdrew to their bunker. The Partisans burnt both houses, but they were not able to occupy the bunker. The Home Defense men who survived left and were posted to the Gorenja vas post.

The 1st Battalion of the Partisan Gorenjski Detachment attacked the post in Lesce on August 6th, 1944 but were unsuccessful. Later the post was moved to Brezje. On May 8th, 1944 the Partisans attacked the post in Gorenja vas. They repeated the attack on September 25th, and again on October 20th, when they also blocked the post in Škofja Loka. On December 18th, 1944 the post was encircled for the fourth time, but the Partisans never succeeded in breaking into the post. On December 6th, 1944 the Partisans attacked the posts in Lučine and Suhi Dol. The Home Guard men from the 43th Company from Št Jošt lent their support, including a heavy mortar, and helped the Gorenjska Home Defense post to repel the Partisan attack. The

Partisans were attacking the post for four days and came very close to penetrating the concertina wire.

The Partisan "Gradnik" and "Prešeren" Brigade confiscated the food and cattle in the villages. The Germans who were at the post did not allow the Home Defense men to patrol the territory because that would weaken the defendability of the post. Morale was low and the Home Defense men complained that they would leave the post because they felt useless. Among the men were many farmers who had to sit back and watch the Partisans take away their property. The attack on the Gorenja vas post was one of the last operations of a four-month long offensive of the 9th Partisan Corps against the Home Guard in Dolomiti (the hills 30km to the west from Ljubljana). The "Vojkova" and "Gradnikova" Brigade and "Škofjeloški" Detachment attacked the post, but due to a thick fog they were not able to press home their attack.

The "Prešern" Brigade was to block the road to Gorenja vas. From Škofja Loka the Germans were advancing with three tanks and seven trucks full of infantry in the direction of Poljane. The Partisans destroyed both bunkers in front of the Gorenja vas post and came close to the post. On December 20th, a German patrol arrived at Gorenja vas and the Partisans had to retreat. The Partisans had 23 soldiers killed and the Home Defense men reported two dead and fourteen wounded. From October 4th-6th, 1944 the Partisans unsuccessfully attacked the post in Cerklje. The "Šlander" Brigade arrived from Styria on October 3rd. At the same time the 3rd Partisan Battalion was raised in the "Kokrški" Detachment. The "Šlander" Brigade did not succeed in contacting the "Kokrški" Partisan Detachment, and the Partisan unit was not strong enough to defeat the Home Defense. In the nearby village Zalog the "Šlandrova" Brigade fought the Chetniks. Both sides had some dead and wounded.

On December 3rd, 1944 the post at Kovor prevented a Partisan attack by the 2nd & 3rd Battalions of the "Kokrški" Detachment. On December 20th, 1944 the Partisans encircled the post in Sopotnica. On March 8th, 1945 the "Prešernova" Brigade occupied the post Sveti Križ. Since the end of February, 1945 the Home Defense fortified a new post near the church at Sveti Križ. It would threaten the Partisan couriers' path as well as the transport of food for the Partisan units in the Slovene Littoral. The Home Defense could control all the villages for more than 20km around. 60 Home Defense men lived in nearby Kališče and prepared the post at Sv. Križ. They built four bunkers, the church, and the bunkers were connected with trenches. Then the "Prešernova" Brigade attacked the post. The "Gradnikova" Brigade, "Jeseniško-bohinjski" Detachment and "Škofjeloški" Detachment, plus two Italian [Partisan] brigades: "Antonio Gramsci" and "Triestina", lent their support.

The Partisans were surprised because the Home Defense abandoned the post and their positions very quickly and thus the Partisans were not able to encircle the post in time to trap them. The men from the post came down to the valley and went to Škofja Loka. Later they were transferred to Škofja Loka, Sopotnica and the Žabnica post. Afterwards the men from the post were considered unreliable and had to be stationed in German posts because they had abandoned the post at Sv. Križ to the Partisans without firing a shot. Records on the casualties incurred by both sides at Sv. Križ are contradictary. The Home Defense states that they had one soldier killed and the Partisans two dead and five wounded, but the Partisan records state that the Home Defense had ten dead and five men were captured.

Also at the post of Kamna Gorica the men did not feel at ease as Partisan reports quoted: *"If they do not get reinforcements they will leave the post and make a post somewhere else. At night they do not sleep in the post but spent the night in private houses."*

The Wounded, Dead and Discharged

The Center Headquarters of the Upper Carnolia Home Defense had sent all posts, special forms where dead soldiers had to be registered. They also had to make a separate list for people who died because they had been tortured to death by the Partisans. The Commander of the post and two witnesses had to sign that form. A few domobranci died during the assault on the Home Defense post at Hotavlje. In November, 1944 an organizer of Home Defense in Škofja Loka was killed, Rudolf Humer. He was getting off the bus when his gun accidentally went off and he killed himself. Humer was burried in Kranj. On November 19th, 1944 there was a funeral in Suha for five domobranci who were killed during the march on Trstenik[48].

Some domobranci also died in hospitals. A statistical report for the period from November 25th to January 10th, 1945 states that 19 domobranci died in hospitals, mostly from their wounds. On March 10th Lance-Sergeant Janez Habjan died, who had led the sally out of the post in Sveti Križ. There were also some cases when the domobranci shot at each other. During the war there were no more than 50 members of the Upper Carnolia Home Defense who died in battles against the Partisans.

---

[48] Actually, ten Home Defense men were killed, among them was a Gorenjska Chetnik.

The Home Defense men could be discharged from service for various offenses. It has been noted that some Home Defense men would return to the post shortly after they would be discharged for an offense. Some men who were ill were sent home. Some men were discharged because they had problems with their eyesight. One of the reasons to leave the Home Defense post was also if the man was not on the post near his home town. A patrol from Cerklje found three Home Defense men who had deserted from the post. They were sent to prison in Brdo. A man was discharged because whenever he was drunk, he would create problems on the post. Some men deserted and joined the Partisans, mostly the ones who were forcibly mobilized into the Home Defense units.

Propaganda

One of the most important propaganda media were newspapers. Most of the magazines and newspapers came to Upper Carnolia from Ljubljana. At the end of 1944, the Home Defense published a newspaper *"Zlatorog"* (Golden Horn). Partisan sources estimated that the circulation was around 15,000 issues and was financed by the German Propaganda office from Bled. The magazine had 16 pages, and at least ten photos. It also informed the readers on the situation on the fronts. In Kranj, Cerklje and Tržič the Home Defense men printed a small newsletter, "Gorenjski domobranec." It consisted of up to four pages and gave information on the Home Defense. In February, 1945 a newspaper, "Gorenjec" was printed by Gorenjska založba in Kranj. Over 10 different newspapers came out of Ljubljana. Radio Ljubljana emitted each Sunday at 11.30 a.m. and each evening at 7 p.m.

The theatre groups played different propaganda plays. After ten years, "Bloody Spain" was still showing.[49] In Cerklje there was even a tambora orchestra. On the posts there were also curators who occasionally said mass in churches. Since 1941 when all the priests were expelled from their parishes, there were only a few Slovene and German priests. Curator Viktor Zorman was in the posts under the Krvavec Mountain. In November, 1944 they promised that a German priest would be exchanged for a Slovene and would lead the divine service and a course for the children in the Slovene language. The Germans also aware of the meaning of propaganda!

In a report from the post at Vodice, the German commander stated that a priest could do more harm to the communists than 10,000

---

[49] A play about the Spanish Civil War.

German soldiers. The Domobranci followed the slogan "Mother, Fatherland, God. Home Guard dogma went as follows:
"Our Mother is a governess who inculcates love for parents and the homeland. Beautiful is our fatherland, with mountains, lakes and cornfields. Everyone should be aware that the existence of our nation is based on a healthy family, with a community in harmony, an animated faith, and the duty of everyone is to stand in the fight against the anti-nation Communists and Jewish plutocracy."
On Eastern Monday of 1945 an anti-Communist mass was held in Šmarna gora, a hill about 7 km north of Ljubljana. In July, 1944 the Gorenjski domobranci had joined an anti-Communist rally in Polhov Gradec and were greeted by General Leon Rupnik. In August 1944 there was a second rally in Črni Vrh. *SS-Oberscharfuehrer* Rudolf Hummer spoke in the meaning on the consequences of Bolshewism in Gorenjska. Among the *Gorenjski domobranci* were several poets. The poet, Ivan Hribovšek from Radovljica, avoided the call-up into the German Army and joined the Home Defense post at Brezje, but later was transferred to the post at Kamna Gorica. After the war Hribovšek was turned over to the Partisans and was never seen again. He wrote mostly lyrical poems. A curator, Viktor Zorman wrote for the monthly's Bogoljub, Dom in svet and Slovenčev koledar. A commander of the post at Luče was an architect. He was with the Village Guard, then was caught by the Partisans and sent to the Partisan Hospital. He deserted to Styria and became a Home Defense man there as well. After the war he studied art in Italy and then emigrated to Argentina.

Retreat and the End of the War

The Germans began a big offensive in March, 1945 in the region of the 9th Partisan Corps. The Chetniks and domobranci also took part in this- one of the very last German anti-partisan offensives. After the end of the offensive only detachments and reserve military units remained. The "Prešern" Brigade remained in the Italian Littoral, while the "Šlandrova" Brigade went on to take part in the final battles in Carinthia. On May, 4th, 1945 the "Kokrški" Detachment liberated prisoners from the prison in Begunje. The "Jeseniško-bohinjski" Detachment moved on to operate in the Ziljska valley, in Austria. Friedrich Rainer, whose headquarters was now in Triest, only decreed the annexation of the Gorenjska province to the Ljubljana province on May 5th, 1945. By May 11th, 1945 all of the Gorenjska province was liberated. After the withdrawal of the German and domobranci units from Gorenjska, the 29th "Hercegovska" Partisan Division entered the province.

At the anniversary of the foundation of the *Slovensko domobranstvo*, General Roesener appointed Leon Rupnik as Inspector General of the Slovensko domobranstvo in September, 1944. The National Committee (Narodni odbor - NO) had accepted a decree establishing a Slovene National Army during a meeting held on January 21st, 1945. The Slovensko domobranstvo would henceforth change its name into the Ljubljana Division, Chetniks units along with Chetniks from Styria would be included into the Drava Detachment, while the SNVZ would be called the Primorski Detachment, and the Upper Carniola Home Defense would be redesignated as the *Gorska Divizija*[50].

On April 6th, 1945 the National Committee appointed into the Headquarters of the Ljubljana Division, the officers who had been in the organizing headquarters of the *Slovensko domobranstvo*. On April 17th, 1945 the National Committee[51] decided that it was very important to thwart the general withdrawal of the Domobranci and the Germans. In the NO many members were not of the same opinion about whether to retreat, or even where and when to leave the country,if at all. In any case, a special board prepared everything for the evacuation. The NO wanted the Slovene National Army sould introduce itself to the western Allies as friends and allies. But they were not sure whether or not the allies would come to Slovenia.

General Roesener discharged the Organizing Headquarters on May 2nd, 1945 and turned over the supreme leadership to Leon Rupnik. He in turn, gave it the next day to the NO. The purpose of the assembly in Sokolski dom and in Ljubljana was to proclaim the Slovene National State within the framework of the Kingdom of Yugoslavia. For the post of President of the Parliament, a newspaper man, Franc Kremžar, was appointed. The leadership of the SNV was given to Colonel Franc Krener who was promoted to the rank of Brigadier-General. The Slovene National Army was to be a part of King Peter's Yugoslav Army in the Fatherland[52]. They accepted a manifesto which stated, among other things, the following: *"Long live King Peter II, long live the Federated Kingdom of Yugoslavia, long live the National State of Slovenia!"*[53]

On April 6th, 1945 the NO appointed officers to the SNV, promoted them and appointed commanders. Anton Mehle was appointed commander of the *Gorska Divizija*, while the Chief of Staff was Milko

---

[50] Mountain Division.

[51] Hereafter referred to as the "NO".

[52] This means that the Slovenian nationalists wished their country to remain in a non-Communist, royalist Yugoslavia

[53] Slovenec, 4. 5. 1945, Ljubljana

Pirih, and the head of the Intelligence Service was headed by Ernest Hirschegger. Initially the Slovene National Army[54] only accepted into its ranks only the active domobranci, officers and Chetniks but because of existing links to the *Slovenska legija*[55] they also comprised their organizers who were not in domobran uniform. Many NCO's who were commanders of the Upper Carniola Home Defense posts were also members of the *Sokolska legija*.

In Ljubljana, crowds converged from all parts of Slovenia. There were many thousands of refugees. On May 5th, 1945 the members of the SNV consented that a general retreat should begin. The *Gorska divizija* was to have collaborated with the *Ljubljana divizija* on the right banks of the Sora and Sava River, while the Drava Odred would be on the left banks of the Savinja and Sava River. The 33rd Batallion of the 12th Brigade defended Kranj. They were to control communication and the villages around Kranj. In Kranj the Intelligence Center of the SNV was to be organized. Especially exposed was the role of post commander who had to look after following the the order to withdraw and restrain his men and himself against any last-minute personal or political revenge against anyone person or group before they withdrew. This included sacking and violence of any kind. The posts were to be supplied with arms and food in advance of their detarture. The head of the Medical Service gave instructions that each civilian or soldier should have with him all necessary hygienic items as well as a first aid kit.

On May 6th, 1945 the Partisans took over Grosuplje and the domobran units withdrew from Novo mesto to Zidani most. On May 7th the order for the general retreat of all domobran units from Ljubljana Province was given. The order to retreat the *Gorska divizija* was given by Major Marko Bitenc. Brigadier-General Frank Krener handed over the leadership of the *Ljubljana divizija* to Lieutenant Milko Vizjak. The Upper Carnolia Home Defense units were led by Major Anton Mehle. They withdrew to Kranj and then towards the Loibl Pass.

On May 9th, 1945 the Partisans captured a train with wounded domobranci. They took them back to Ljubljana from Lesce, 5 kilometers from Radovljica in Upper Carnolia. Most of them were killed. A few hundred people were captured by the Partisans around the Drava Bridge near Borovlje. Some 500 people were captured on their retreat near Tržič. The locals were hostile towards the retreating people and threw bricks at them. Partisan units were attacking the formations with

---

[54] Hereafter referred to as the SNV.
[55] Slovene Legion.

all types of artillery and howitzers, and many people lost their lives but the lucky ones, only their meager possesions.

The Chetniks were reorganized near the Loibl Pass. Together with the nearest Home Defense unit from Kovor, they withdrew into Carinthia. German units only allowed militry formations to pass through the tunnel, while the civilians had to cross the peak of the mountain. On May 11th, some Chetniks shot the German frontier guard post and a crowd of people rushed through the tunnel. The Partisans continued to shoot at retreating columns. Guides who were among the tired people encouraged them to move faster and to keep in some sort of rank and file.

The Partisan *"Bračič" Brigade* and the *"Koroški" Detachment* received the task of defending the pass over the Drava River into Austria. They fought with domobran units on May 10th, 1945. Because of the large numbers of Home Guard forces, the 3rd Batallion of the *"Koroški" Detachment* was forced to withdraw westwards. Desperate to escape, the Home Guard had thrown into the assault 17 tanks and two entire domobran assault battalions. The 1st Battalion of the *"Bračič" Partisan Brigade* was defeated and was pushed towards the Drava River. From the "Bračič" and "Koroški" Partisan Detachments, about 180 soldiers were killed, while the Armed Group of Motorized Detachment of the 4th Partisan Army lost four tanks and had 15 soldiers killed.

After the battle near the town of Borovlje the representatives of the SNV and NO travelled to Klagenfurt to the headquarters of the local British Army units, to discuss their situation[56]. In Viktring a list of all members of the SNV was made in triplicate. One was sealed up and sent back with komora (tren), one copy was taken with the units, while the third was in the hands of Mirko Bitenc. He burnt this copy on May 31st, 1945 when it became clear to him that the English were forcibly handing over the domobranci to the Partisans in Slovenia.

The Chetniks had kept their weapons until they came to Vikting field. In Borovlje they introduced themselves as Mihailović's Chetniks, but more than 13,000 domobranci before them had to hand in their arms. Major Mirko Bitenc thought that a group should go back to Upper Carnolia and prepare a base for further resistance. The SNV reorganzied the batallions, regiments and divisions. The Commander was still Franc Krener. The 5th Regiment was known as the Upper Carnolia Regiment. The commander of the I[st] Batallion was Milko Pirih. On May 24th, the domobranci from Novo mesto arrived at Viktring. The majority had not gotten through, but had been caught by the Partisans in Lower Carnolia, in the Krka River Valley.

---

[56] In effect, their fate.

In Krško (Gurk) the rest of the officers asked their soldiers and their families to choose whether they wished to go on to Carinthia or if they would prefer to go home. A smaller group decided to go to Carinthia. Soldiers and civilians prepared shelters to live on Viktring field. A post from Smlednik had brought an entire kitchen unit with them. The camp was opened to everyone. Many dealers came and the people traded the last precious things which they had for food. In the civilian camp there were still 1,262 men, 414 women, and 460 children from Upper Carnolia as of May 31st, 1945. Those numbers were reported after the majority of the Upper Carnolia Home Defense had been sent back to Yugoslavia.

In the camp at Viktring rumors soon developed which said that the English would soon take them to Italy. As a matter of fact the Upper Carnolia Home Defense members had been told during the retreat from Slovenia that they would return in 14 days! On May 24th, the first transports left, persumably bound for Italy. The Partisans came onto the train in Maria Elm. With the first transport were sent also 20 carts of archives from the Slovenian Home Guard. Transports were leaving every day. On May 27th the first groups left for Slovenia. On May 28th the Upper Carnolia domobranci left Viktring field. About 60 Chetniks and the commander of the Upper Carnolia Chetnik Deteachment, Milko Pirih also went with them. The train stopped at the Škofja Loka railway station. The domobranci were taken to the castle and were arranged into rooms on the post base. On June 14th they were sent on foot to Šentvid, about 30 km near Ljubljana. On August 6th-7th, 1945 many were sent to Kočevje and killed.

On June 13th, 1945 the representatives of the camp communities at Viktring sent a document to the English government in London, in which they asked for help for the soldiers who were in the prisons in Škofja Loka and Ljubljana. A few men escaped from the transports and returned to the camp in Viktring but nobody would believe that the English were sending back to Yugoslavia the soldiers. On 31st May 31st inspite of the notices that the transports were being diverted to Yugoslavia, about 500 men decided to follow their companions. On June 2nd the transports were stopped. The domobranci who stayed at Viktring wanted to organize a group to help their comrades in Slovenian prisons. They sent some groups to investigate the situation into Slovenia but soon found out that it was already too late. The camps and the castles where the domobranci were kept, were too well guarded. By the end of June, 1945 the Viktring camp was disbanded. The refugees were sent to Pegezz-Lienz, Spittal, Šentvid ob Glini and Liechtenstein near Judenburg.

The Situation in Upper Carnolia After May 15th, 1945

More than a year after the end of war, organized groups of domo-branci still operated in Upper Carnolia. They also came across from Carinthia and performed sabotage activities. Near Radovljica there were about 30 to 40 men who were former domobranci and who maintained contacts with the men who came over the Karawanken Alps. In the Autumn of 1945, surrounding the region of Kranj, there were 50 men who were organized into groups. Groups of former *Gestapo* and *Gegenbande* men were also seen. A group of 100 men attacked a Partisan patrol of the Narodna obramba near Tržič. In the mountains of Pokljuka a group of 60 domobranci were caught. In the forest under Mežakla, 200 domobranci were operating. They were led by Andrej Noč, a former *Gestapo* member. In the beginning of August 1945 there were about 660 men of different formations still wandering around, trying to come over the border. Up until September, 1945 Partisan units had caught over 2,000 men. In the summer of 1946 there were more groups still operating, but altogether it turned out that their numbers were only 92 men.

At the end of the war, numerous Upper Carnolia Home Defense men and their families fled to Carinthia. At least 1,000 of them were returned by the English. They withdrew in order, leaving Viktring field as a formation of the SNV. The percentages from the various posts were as follows: From Cerklje 25%, Domžale 25%, Škofja Loka 30%, Tupaliče 20%, and from Lučine 31% of the men were sent back to Slovenia. Checking the data regarding their birth dates, some had written the presume date of death: *"razglašen za mrtvega, ...dan , ki ga pogrešani ni preživel"* (proclaimed dead,.... the day that the missing did not survive). The dates of their death are listed as diffe-rent days between 1945 and 1946. Among them are men of various ages, but younger men, those born in 1926 were released as a rule. The youngest Home Defense soldier who was killed, was born in 1929! So there was actually no rule as to who would be killed and who would survive. Often it all depended on the members of the Local People's [Communist] Committee - *Krajevni ljudski odbor* – or KLO.

At the end of war about 100 Slovenians who had served in the German Army, and had later served in the Home Defense, and had withdrawn into Carinthia, were handed over to Partisans by the English. The majority of them were from Kovor, Tupaliče and the Brezje post and one third of all who were returned were from those posts. In Domžale, ex-German Army Slovenes represented 1/4 of all who were returned. Information was collected for 70 soldiers. 21 of them were pronounced dead. It is estimated that the total number of

Upper Carnolia Home Defense men killed were about 800. There are still about 200 Home Defense men who are still alive.

In some villages all Home Defense men were killed. In the district of Škofja Loka the procentage of killed Home Defense men would be 75%. After the amnesty on August 6th, 1945 some domobranci were released. The boards of the Liberation Front (OF) had written, as early as 1944, lists of those who colllaborated with the Germans and were members of different anti-Partisan organizations. This had been done through the *Komisija za ugotavljanje zločinov okupatorjev in njegovih pomagačev* (The Committee to Find War Crimes by the Occupiers and Their Collaborators) which collected piles of the information on crimes and actions of individuals from towns and villages.

The characteristics of the particular domobranci are interesting. 'J.B.' was stationed at the Gorenja vas post. He was a farmer. He was married and had two children. His wife had also fled with him to Carinthia. He did not commit any crimes, and only threatened people. 'A.S.' was also a farmer. He had rank. He had four children. His family fled with him in 1943. He was also among the first to take action. He arrested some people. He fled to Carinthia. After being released, many former Home Defense men never returned home. Different local groups were looking for revenge and caught the released domobranci and killed them. There is not a lot of information on the imprisoned Home Defense men. The reports of the KLO state that the men were in the camps in Teharje or in the castle at Škofja Loka, or were in prisons in Ljubljana, Begunje or in work camps in Kočevje.

The destiny of the leading men in the Center Headquarters of the Upper Carnolia Home Defense and the commanders of the posts were as follows: Erich Dichtl, who had been stationed in Kranj since 1941, had a wife who lived in Villach. In May, 1945 he fled to Carinthia. He met the domobranci at Viktring. Afterwards he was in a camp for war criminals in Spittal. Slavko or Alojz Krek escaped and went underground in February, 1945. The Partisans attacked him and he was sent to a hospital to recuperate. When the *Gestapo* came to arrest him, he fled to his friend's house in Ovsenik, Predoslje, in Upppper Carnolia. At the end of war he went to Klagenfurt and then to his uncle, Minister Miha Krek who was living in Rome, Italy.

Then he studied in Berlin. In May of 1946 he was arrested and sent to to a camp at Wansee. In January, 1947 he was arrested again and sent to Yugoslavia, where he was charged for the crimes, among others, that he participated in *Dijaška protikoministična akcija*, that he was Rupnik's secretary, that he organized sending propaganda material to Upper Carnolia, collaborated with the Chetniks and organized Center Headquarters of the Upper Cranial Home Defense

Force. He was sentenced to life in prison, but was released in the early sixties.

After the war, Milan Amon was in the camp for war criminals in Wolfsberg. After six months he was released. He died in Buenos Aires, Argentina. Franc Erpič now lives in Australia. Most of the commanders of the Home Defense posts were born between the years 1915 to 1925. Twenty-two of them were active only in the Home Defense and did not join either the German Army or the Partisans. They all joined the formation quite soon, in March and April 1944. The commander from Cerklje was married and after the war was sentenced to 20 years in prison. Later the court changed the sentence to death by shooting. He was shot in April, 1946 in Ljubljana.

Some commanders were separated from their men as soon as the train came into Slovenian territory. Just before the end of war, three commanders were killed in action. Peter Cerar, a commander from the Domžale post was killed in mid-April, 1945. He led a patrol and a partisan shot him in the stomach. He was sent to a hospital but died in a few days later of his wound. Franc Juvan, a commander from the post in Vače received a letter to attend the meeting in Dolsko, but the Partisans were waitin for him in an ambush and killed him.

At the end of the war, out of 30 commanders for whom we acquired their records, 14 were handed over to the partisans in Carinthia, 5 of which were proclaimed "dead." Six commanders who did not return to Slovenia survived. The commanders of the posts at Šentvid near Lukovica, Predoslje, Lahoviče emigrated to the United States. After the war, the property of numerous domobranci was confiscated, and they first lost their citizenship and then their property, which was given to *Krajevni urad za narodno imovino*, or KUNI (the Local Office for the People's Property).

Incorporation Into a Socialist Society

After the war many Home Defense men and their relatives were sent to prisons. They were even arrested several times. The authorities forcibly confiscated their cattle from the farms or sent them to youth brigades to build roads, bridges and blocks of houses. About 50 Home Defense men from Gorenjska were sent to Ljubljana prison. Those were mostly the ones who did not go to Carinthia and were arrested in the first days of May, 1945. Sometimes the authorities arrested groups of local people. The men from the villages under Krvavec were arrested for helping people to escape abroad, collaborating with them, illegally crossing the border, hiding German soldiers, "anti-nationalist" activities, espionage and "illegal connections" abroad.

Many who sympathised with the Home Defense had problems finding a job. It often happened that a father went to Carinthia and was sent back, the mother worked alone on the farm, struggled with the authorities and had difficult times. They died of hard work and other hardships. The children who remained alone were looked after by the Red Cross. The mayor of Vodice, a small village 10 kilometers from Ljubljana, sent a letter to a well known writer who was supposed to be a member of a commission for complaints. He wanted to know where were 16 men, all who had been domobranci, from Vodice, and who were turned over to the Partisans. The writer answered that they were presumaby sent to work in southern Yugoslavia. In reality, all of them were already dead.

Conclusions

During World War II, about 130,000 men, women, and children lived in the lower part of Gorenjska. In Domžale, Kamnik, Škofja Loka and Litija district an additional 100,000 people lived there as well. The *"Oberkrainer Selbstschutz" (Gorenjski domobranci)* represented only about 3% of the above-mentioned population figures. Together with the German units stationed in this part of Slovenia, they were strong enough to keep the Partisans hiding in the forests, and most often prevented the guerrilla bands from operating in the wide open spaces of *Gorenjska*. For example, in the Cerklje community lived 4,659 people, only 156 of them were in Partisan units while over 500 of them were in the *Gorenjsko domobranstvo*. Of the estimated 15,000 Partisans which operated at one time or another in the *Gorenjska* Region, about 2,600 were killed. An estimated 3,762 Slovenian men served in the *Gorenjsko domobranstvo*. This number is a bit deceiving, since 2,600 was the highest number of them serving at any one time[57]. The remaining 1,162 men probably ran through the ranks of the unit from one time to another. We must take into account the fact that a military organization enrolls soldiers, then either retains them, or losses some of them through attrition (death, disease, wounds, and "other" losses). In September, 1944 the *Oberkrainer Selbstschutz* numbered more than one thousand men, while in December, 1944 about 1,460 men were stationed in twenty-two separate posts.

By March, 1945 that number had increased to 2,489 men. The recruiting figures given for the latter half of 1944 and the beginning of 1945, when compared with these other strength reports, clearly support the hypothesis that the strength of the *Gorenjsko*

---

[57] May, 1945.

domobranstvo kept rising, at a time when the fortunes were clearly against their German allies. This phenomenon must have an explanation. The simple reason has to be the blind belief that most people had in the Catholic Church in this region, and the anti-Communist ideals that the population felt as a result. This leads us to some final figures on deaths in this region of Slovenia.

About 800 Communist activists lost their lives here during the war, while 350 were victims of Partisan violence, and an additional 1,100 people were shot as hostages of the Nazis. A comparatively trifling number of 10 lives were lost due to "Allied" bombing. When we compare the total number of casualties taken on all sides including the civilian losses, we come up with about 8,000 lives lost in the province of *Gorenjska*. This is about 3.48% of the total pre-war population figures. What does this all mean? The conclusion that can be reached is that most of the heavy fighting was done in other parts of Slovenia and that the "*Oberkrainer Selbstschutz*," together with the German occupation force in Gorenjska, were enough to sufficiently neutralize the [Communist] Partisan Movement in that region until almost the end of the war.

Location of the Posts-

Date	Post Location	Number of all who were ever registered at the posts:
December 1943	Lučine	61
January 1944	Črni vrh	121
January 1944	Suhi Dol	115
	Gorenja vas	63
March 1944	Škofja Loka	157
April 1944	Kranj	120
May 1944	Cerklje	193
	Lahovče	83
	Predoslje	60
June 1944	Hotavlje	
July 1944	Lesce	
	Voklo	93
	Bobovek	32
August 1944	Vodice	68
	Smlednik	141
	Domžale	289
September 1944	Žabnica	59

October 1944	Kovor	46
	Mengeš	68
	Šentvid/Ljubljana	4
	Tupaliče	174
	Udarna četa	102
November 1944	Šentvid/Lukovica	6
	Sopotnica	do 70
	Mavčiče	46
	Brezje	70
December 1944	Goričane	42
	Litija	123
January 1945	Zagorica	
	Vače	84
	Ljubno	
	Luče	
	Jezersko	38
February 1945	Županje Njive	
	Kresnice	
	Bitnje	
	Dolsko	up to 30
	Sv. Križ	up to 60
	Kamna Gorica	
	Ribno	
March 1945	Goriče	
	Tržič	
	Komenda	26
	Preska	up to 15
	Mekinje	
	Stražišče	
April 1945	Kokra	

Register of Volunteers at the Upper Carnolia Home Defense Posts:

1944 January	140
Februar	108
March	168
April	165
May	130

June	100
July	118
August	250
September	170
October	193
November	333
December	271

69

1945 January	410
February	46

Register of Volunteers at the Following Posts:

Cerklje

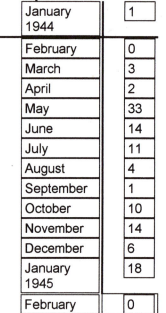

January 1944	1
February	0
March	3
April	2
May	33
June	14
July	11
August	4
September	1
October	10
November	14
December	6
January 1945	18
February	0

Èrni vrh

January 1944	4 3
February	4
March	3 9
April	4
May	1
June	0
July	0
August	0

September	0
October	3
November	2 1
December	3
January 1944	1
February	0

Domžale

Januar 1944	3
February	1 5
March	1
April	2
May	2
June	4
July	4
August	5 4
September	3 2
October	4
November	3 4
December	1 9
January 1945	9 0
February	2

Udarna četa

January 1944	0
February	1
March	1
April	3
May	1

June	8		November	5
July	4		December	6
August	3		January	5
	0		1945	
September	1		February	1
	1			
October	2			
	4			

Town	A	B	C
Brezje	41	32	32
Brdo	11	8	0
Cerklje	43	27	27
Erni vrh	23	0	0
Domzale	126	58	58
Gorenja vas	3	0	0
Kovor	29	24	22
Kranj	28	20	20
Lahoviee	22	9	9
Maveiee	18	9	9
Menges	23	12	12
Smeldnik	31	18	16
Skofja Loka	52	1	0
Tupailee	42	21	19
Vodice	16	8	8
Udarna eeta	38	27	27
Litija	41	11	11
Lueine	6	0	0
Predoslje	24	16	16
Suhi Dol	29	2	0
Vaee	16	7	6
Zabonica	27	13	13

A= former partisans who joined the Home Guard.
B= ex-German Army Inductees who later joined the Home Guard.
C= former ex-German Army inductees, who later became parti-sans, and then joined the Home Guard.

HOME GUARD VOLUNTEERS BY AGE GROUP:

Age Structure

Up to 1900	1900 –1910	1910-1915	1915-1920	1920-1925	1925 +
67	526	357	239	465	347
At Post in	Brezje:				
1	8	5	13	34	13
At Post in	Lahovee:				
9	38	11	8	16	8
At Post in	Lueine:				
5	31	7	3	5	9
At Post in	Udarna eeta	(Assault	Squad):		

71

1	2	9	19	59	9

Soldiers from the posts who were returned from Carinthia:

Brezje	4
Cerklje	57
Črni Vrh	18
Domžale	67
Gorenja vas	19
Kranj	0
Lahoviče	29
Smlednik	21
Škofja Loka	50
Voklo	29
Tupaliče	37
Udarna četa	29
Litija	18
Suhi Dol	47

PHOTOGRAPHIC SECTION
Photographs of the *Gorenjsko Domobranstvo*

These photographs are all very rare and were found just recently through field work. The author of the majority of these photographs (his pseudonym is Janez Gorenc) is still alive and he succeeded in hiding them before he was sent back to Slovenia from Viktring Field on May 28th, 1945. The negatives were given to a friend and he returned them to the author after the war.

1) *SS-Oberscharfuehrer* Erich Dichtl, the head of *Gorenjsko Domobranstvo*. This photo was taken just before the parade in Kranj on September 15th, 1944 All domobran units gathered at the sport ground near the Home Defense barracks in Kranj (Krainburg).
1a) The town of Škofja Loka during World War II. The photo was taken before February, 1942, when the name of the province of *Gorenjska* was changed by Gauleiter Friedrich Rainer from *Suedkaerten* to *Oberkrain*.
1b) The funeral of (most likely), the organizers of the Home Defense in Škofja Loka on March 18th, 1944. In the foreground are two Upper Carnolia Home Defense men acting a honor guards.
1c) Rudolf Humer, organizer of Home Defense in Škofja Loka, is seen here giving the eulogy at the funeral of March 18th, 1944.

2) Two Home Defense men receive the *Verwundeten Abzeichnung* (wound badge), during a ceremony in Kranj, in September, 1944.

3) A parade of the Home Defense through the streets of Kranj, September 15th, 1944. At the head is Erich Dichtl.

4) A Home Defense unit from Kranj, September 1944. All of the men are wearing the same type of Police uniform, but different shirts and ties. The caps are either peaked mountain caps or the caps of the Slovenian Home guard.

5) A Home Defense unit from Cerklje, the men are mostly armed with the Italian Manlicher carbine, the Carcano M-38. The man lying in the middle has an M-24. There are not many officers among them, only one man in the middle (sitting) has the officer's shoulder boards. The man, third in the second row, sitting, wears a *Verwundeten Abzeichen* (wound badge).

6) A Home Defense patrol from Cerklje, Stiška vas, in February 1945. The patrol consists mainly of older men. They are wearing four different types of caps: an ex-Yugoslav soft cover cap, a camouflage cap, ordinary peaked mountain cap, and the third man from the right is wearing a cap of the Slovene Home Guard) Only two wear a proper German military belt. In addition the fourth man, who is a little bit younger than the others, is wearing a badge of the SNV (an eagle), which implies that he could be a *Gorenjski Chetnik*.

7) Domobranci from the post at Gorenja vas. The caps they are wearing are varied. Some have caps worn by the *Slovensko domobranstvo,* with the oval cockade showing the Slovenian tricolor superimposed by a single headed eagle. One man, the second from the left (sitting) is wearing a Slovene Home Guard emblem.

8) Home Defense men from Sopotnica during a patrol in February, 1945.

9) Home Defense with local townspeople from Kremenk.

10) A guard in front of the Škofja Loka post. A man is also wearing the oval Slovene tricolor cockade on his *Feldmutze.* Resting on the stool, by the guard is a book for sale entitled "Èrne bukve." This book details all of the people who were killed by the Partisans.

11) A guard on the Sopotnica post, controlling the access to the post and the way to Poljane Valley. In these hills were important Partisan paths through *Gorenjska* to the Slovene Littoral.

12) The leaders of the Sopotnica post. On the right is commander Habjan, in the middle a Slovene Home Guard curator from Ljubljana. The officer on the left is wearing a camouflage jacket of unusal pattern. It does not appear to be of German or Italian in origin, and may in fact be one of those British camouflage materials captured by the Home Guard and tailored into a jacket. The photo was taken in February, 1945.

13) The men from the Sopotnica Post in February, 1945.

14) Home Guard men in front of a bunker at the Sopotnica Post, February, 1945.

15) A Home Defense patrol from Sopotnica, February 1945

16) Another patrol from Sopotnica. The man on the left is carrying an M37 machine gun. This photo was also taken in February, 1945.

17) A patrol from Sopotnica. A Slovene Home Guard curator is also with them, as the Headquarters of the Slovene Home Guard recommended that curators should wear the Home Guard uniform and be comissioned with an officer's rank. The leading man is the commander of the post and the second is his deputy, who is wearing a camouflage jacket. This photo was also taken in February, 1945.

18) Yet another photo (taken in February, 1945) of a patrol from Sopotnica. The second man from the left is a Slovene Home Guard curator wearing a winter camouflage jacket.

19) A funeral of the *Gorenjska* Home Defense in Suha, in November, 1944.

20) Funeral procession of domobran Peter Jagodic, December 1944.

21) A commander of the Sopotnica Post, and the war curator from Škofja Loka, seen here in civilian clothes.

22) The Home Defense post at Sopotnica, which was established in November, 1944 in the mountains above Zminc, 10km from Škofja Loka.

23) A guard at the Sopotnica Post, February 1945.

24) A *Gorenjska* Home Defense man from Apno. He wears the cap of the Slovene Home Guard, without any cockade. His weapon is an Italian machine gun, the Breda model 30 light machine gun. This photo was taken in the summer of 1944.

24a) A Home Guard in front of his home village in Valburga near Smlednik. The beauty of the Slovenian countryside in winter is clearly seen by this photo.

24b) Quite a rare uniform for a Home Defense soldier. This volunteer has managed to acquire what looks like an early pattern Waffen-SS camouflage smock. He has sewn the cloth emblem of the *Gorenjska* Home Defense on the left sleeve of the camo tunic. His "uniform" is completed with black, civilian trousers and a pullover sweater.

25) An anti-Communist meeting at Šmarna gora in April, 1945.

26) Aother photo taken of that same meeting at Šmarna gora, in April, 1945.

Photos 27) to 30) A squad of officer candidates march through the snow while attending an officer candidate course held at Brdo, in a property that contained a castle in a large estate that once belonged to the Karadjordjeviæ family. The course lasted 14 day. This photo was taken in February, 1945.

31) The leaders of the course, which included the head, Franc Rigler, who came from the Slovene Home Guard post in Dravlje near Ljubljana (third from the left). All the other men in this photo wear caps worn by the Slovene Home Guard.

32) The entire group of men who attended the course at Brdo in February, 1945.

33) This certificate was given to the men who completed the course. The emblem of the *Gorenjsko Domobranstvo* is clearly visible, in red and white colours with a blue eagle and blue trimming. They were awarded the certificate which indicated that they finished the course. The date when they attended it was also given. The grade which they achieved in comparison with all other participants in the course was also shown.

34) The cover page of the magazine of the *Gorenjsko domobranstvo* "Zlatorog," or Golden Horn. This name was chosen for the Golden Horned wild goats which roamed the Gorenjska region.

35) Home Guard troops and civilians withdrawing from *Gorenjska*. Long columns were seen leaving the country- all heading towards Loibl Tunnel and Carinthia in May, 1945.

36) This photo was taken at Viktring Field in May, 1945. The crowded conditions of the camp can be clearly seen.

37) Men from a *Gorenjska* Home Defense post waiting for bread at Viktring Field, May 1945.

38) & 39) A column of Home Guard and Home Defense men who were handed over to Partisans are seen arriving in Kranj, on May 30th, 1945. Partisan guards can be seen escorting them.

40) The men from the Skofja Loka Post. The interesting thing about this photograph is that two of these men (first & third from the left, standing) are wearing the death's head emblem on the front of their *feldmutze* (soft cover). This was not according to regulations, which required the men to wear the oval tricolor cockade in place of the Death's Head emblem. What was regulation, was the use of the SS cloth eagle and swastika on the left side of the *Feldmutze*.

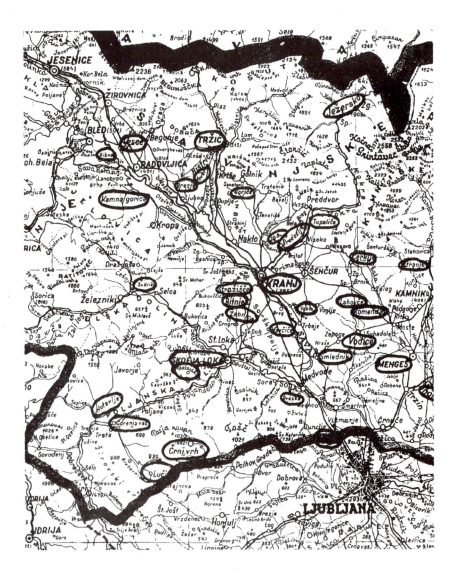

The above map lists the Home Guard posts in western Gorenjsko. The thick border at the top is the Austrian border. Ljubljana province is similarly outlined at the bottom of the map.

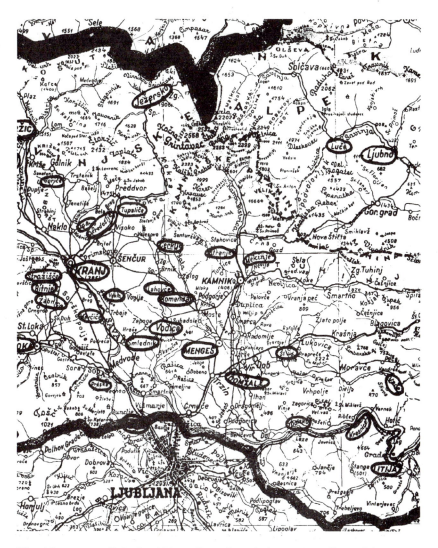

The above map lists the Home Guard posts in eastern Gorenjsko.
Once again, the thick border on top delineates the frontier with Austria,
while the thick border on the bottom of the map shows the border with
Ljubljana Province. To the east, the border between Styria and Upper
Carnolia (Gorenjsko) can be seen with a thin line.

Die organisatorische Aufstellung des Oberkrainer Selbstschutzes lautet

a/Kommandeur der Sicherheitspolizei und des SD Veldes,
   SS-Obersturmbannf.P e r s t e r e r.

b/Als Führer für den Oberkrainer Selbstschuts wurde
   SS-Oberscharf.D i c h t l,Krainburg,beauftragt

c/Als Beauftragter für die politische Linie
   SS-Obersturmf.M e s s n e r,Krainburg.

d/Als Beauftragte für die Finanzierung und Verwaltung,für die
   in den Stapobereichen liegenden Selbstschutz-Stützpunkte,die
   von den Aussenstellenleitern bestimmten Beamten.

e/Der verantwortliche Chef des Zentrums des Oberkrainer Selbst-
   schutzes innerhalb der Selbstschutz-Stützpunkte ist K r e k
   Slavko,welcher im engsten Einvernehmen mit SS-Obersturmf.
   Messner und mir zu handeln hat.

f/Für die militärische und disziplinarische Ausbildung sämtlicher
   Stützpunkte in Oberkrain,habe ich Herrn F l u d e r n i k bestimmt.

g/Für den Nachrichtendienst innerhalb sämtlicher Stützpunkte in
   Oberkrain ist Herr O v s e n i k Johann bestimmt.

h/Die Propaganda übernimmt Herr P e r n e Alois.

i/Die kriminalistischen Untersuchungen,OF und NOV-Bandenorganisa-

Above: Part of a five-page document from the Commander of the Sipo and SD in Veldes, detailing the organizational command structure of the *Oberkrainer Selbstschutzes* (*Gorenjsko domo-branstvo*).

APPENDIX I – Slovenian Volunteers Under Gestapo Auspices

[This appendix was written by Antonio J. Munoz and originally appeared in "Slovenian Axis Forces in World War II 1941-1945" $22, Axis Europa Books, 1996. This book is a comprehensive history of ALL Slovenian collaborationist forces, beginning with Italian supported units and ending with German sponsored formations. It comes with full color plates by famed military artist, Vincent Wai. Still available from the publisher]

On January 9th, 1944 the German *Gestapo* (short for *Geheim Staatspolizei,* or State Secret Police) formed about 1,000 Slovenian volunteers from the annexed province of Upper Carnolia *(Oberkrain).* This was the former Slovene province of *Gorenjsko.* Previously, only ethnic Germans had been allowed to form armed units in this province and in the province of *Untersteiermark* (*Stajerska* in Slovenian, called Lower Styria in English). But the necessities of war softened the attitude of the Germans.

The force was assigned a nominal Slovenian commander, who was initially Slavko Krek, but when he was killed, that title went to Franc Erpic. In reality, it was led and organized by a charismatic Austrian *Gestapo Scharfuehrer* (sergeant) named Erich Dichtl. Dichtl had the ability of speaking the local (Slovenian) language fluently, and as a result, the Slovenian *Gestapo* volunteers were more prone to trusting and accepting him as one of their own. This was important with regards to their effectiveness. The *Gestapo* force was dubbed the *"Gorenjsko domobranstvo"* (the Upper Carnolia Home Defense Force), but in the German language this title translated to "Oberkrainer Selbstschutz", so it was also referred to by this name.

The headquarters of the "Oberkrainer Selbstschutz" was in the city of Kranj (Krainburg). Sergeant Dichtl was methodical in his planning, and by the end of 1944 he had enlarged his command to include twenty (20) fortified towns and hamlets, with an average of perhaps 80-100 men apiece. In October, 1944 he gathered between 100-150 of the most physically fit and best qualified men from these posts (which now numbered about 2,000 volunteers) and formed them into a special *Gestapo* Assault Company. The mission of this elite unit was to hunt down the Partisan bands.

Dichtl's force proved to be quite effective, so much so that by May, 1945 it had been enlarged to a force of 2,600 men and forty-six (46) fortified posts! This force was designated as one of the three Slovenian nationalist "divisions" of what would turn out to be the still-born Slovene National Army- a force that was declared into existence on May 4th, 1945. It is very intriguiging to speculate how a *Gestapo* led, armed, and trained military force could have been considered a part of this pro-Western "Slovene National Army." But to the Slovenian nationalists, it didn't seem to dawn on them that perhaps the Western Allies would have second (or third) thoughts about accepting into their "protection" a unit that had been formed by such a blatantly Nazi organization as the *Gestapo!*

1] FORGOTTEN LEGIONS: OBSCURE COMBAT FORMATIONS OF THE WAFFEN-SS, 1943-1945 ISBN- 0-87364-646-0 Hard Cover Book. 424 pp. $25 (FEBRUARY, 2000)

2] THE KAMINSKI BRIGADE: A HISTORY, 1941-1945. ISBN- 1-891227-02-5 Soft Cover 64 pp $20

3] LIONS OF THE DESERT: ARAB VOLUNTEERS IN THE GERMAN ARMY, 1941-1945 ISBN- 1-891227-03-3 36pp $18

4] SLOVENIAN AXIS FORCES IN WORLD WAR II, 1941-1945 ISBN- 1-891227-04-1 Soft Cover 84pp $22

5] FOR CROATIA & CHRIST: THE CROATIAN ARMY IN WORLD WAR II, 1941-1945 O/P

6] HERAKLES & THE SWASTIKA: GREEK VOLUNTEERS IN THE GERMAN ARMY, POLICE & SS, 1943- 1945 O/P

7] FORGOTTEN LEGIONS BOOKLET ISBN- 1-891227-06-8 Soft Cover $25

8] THE HUNGARIAN ARMY & ITS MILITARY LEADERSHIP IN WWII ISBN- 1-891227-08-4 88pp Soft Cover, $25

9] HITLER'S EASTERN LEGIONS, Volume I - THE BALTIC SCHUTZMANNSCHAFT ISBN- 1-891227-09-2 96pp, Soft Cover, $21

10] HITLER'S EASTERN LEGIONS, Volume II - THE OSTTRUPPEN ISBN- 1-891227-10-6 56pp, Soft Cover, $24

SPECIAL: Buy BOTH Hitler's Eastern Legions, Volumes I & II for ONLY $31 !!!!!

11] THE GERMAN POLICE ISBN- 1-891227-11-4 442pp, Soft Cover, $42

12] EASTERN TROOPS IN ZEELAND, THE NETHERLANDS, 1943-1945 ISBN- 1-891227-00-9 101pp, Soft Cover, $28

13] RUSSIAN VOLUNTEERS IN HITLER'S ARMY, 1941-1945 ISBN- 1-891227-01-7 60pp, Soft Cover, $13

14] HRVATSKI ORLOVI: PARATROOPERS OF THE INDEPENDENT STATE OF CROATIA, 1942-45 ISBN- 1-891227-13-0 Hard Cover, 70pp, $22

15] CHETNIK: The Story of the Royal Yugoslav Army of the Homeland, 1941-1945 ISBN- 1-891227-20-3 Soft Cover, 64pp, $18

16] THE ROYAL HUNGARIAN ARMY 1920-1945 Volume I Organization & History ISBN- 1-891227-19-X Hard Cover, 318pp, $55

17] MUSSOLINI'S AFRIKA KORPS: The Italian Army in North Africa, 1940-1943 ISBN 1-891227-14-9 Hard Cover, 220pp, $36

18] IRON FIST: A Combat History of the 17th SS Panzer Grenadier Division 'Gotz von Berlichingen', 1944-45" ISBN 1-891227-29-7 Soft Cover, 84pp, $20

19] "GESTAPO VOLUNTEERS: The Oberkrainer Selbstschutz, 1943-1945" ISBN 1-891227-30-0 $20

20] "For Czar & Country: A History of the Russian Guard Corps, 1941-1945" ISBN 1-891227-23-8 $13

UPCOMING BOOKS: We have FOUR (4) books which are upcoming, but we do not have definitive dates of publication. We can tell you though, that they are in various stages of development.

21] "Goring's Grenadiers: The Luftwaffe Field Divisions, 1942-1945"

22] "ENEMIES ON ALL SIDES: The Croatian Armed Forces, 1941-1945" Volume I – Army, Navy & Air Force

23] "DECIMA X MAS: The Italian Naval Commandos & the Italian Social Republic, 1943-1945"

We accept ALL MAJOR CREDIT CARDS:

VISA, MASTERCARD, DISCOVER, AMERICAN EXPRESS. Shipping and Handling charges apply. Please visit our web site at http://www.axiseuropa.com for a full explanation.

Axis Europa Books, 53-20 207th Street, Bayside NY 11364 USA
Phone (718) 423-9893 Fax (718) 229-1352

Picture 1

Picture 1A

Picture 1B

Picture 1C

Picture 2

Picture 3

Picture 4

Picture 5

Picture 6

Picture 7

Picture 8

Picture 9

Picture 10

Picture 12

Picture 13

Picture 14

Picture 15

Picture 16

Picture 17

Picture 18

Picture 19

Picture 20

Picture 21

Picture 22

Picture 23

Picture 24

Picture 24A

Picture 24B

Picture 25

Picture 26

Picture 27

Picture 28

Picture 29

Picture 30

Picture 31

Picture 32

SPRIČEVALO

iz _____ je v času od _____ do _____ 194__

obiskoval desetarski tečaj v Poveljstvu tečajev Gorenjskega

Domobranstva in ga završil z _____ uspehom.

Na podlagi izpitnih ocen je dosegel izmed _____ tečajnikov

_____ mesto.

Imenovani je usposobljen za _____ .

Kranj - Brdo, _____ 194 .

Picture 33

15. / I. 1945

ZLATOROG

Picture 35

Picture 36

Picture 37

Picture 38

Picture 39

Picture 40